ne

oy

ni
Laura Lee
Caterina Frisone
Edwin Heathcote
Niall McLaughlin
Lily Jencks

In the memory of Charles Jencks

Maggie's centres

Maggie's centres

editorial project
Forma Edizioni srl
Florence, Italy
redazione@formaedizioni.it
www.formaedizioni.it

editorial direction
Laura Andreini

author
Caterina Frisone

editorial staff
Maria Giulia Caliri
Raffaele Moretti
Beatrice Papucci
Elena Varani

graphic design
Isabella Peruzzi

translations
Sylvia Notini
Katy Hannan
Karen Whittle

photolitography
Forma Edizioni

texts by
Laura Andreini
Laura Lee
Caterina Frisone
Edwin Heathcote
Niall McLaughlin
Lily Jencks

First Edition: May 2022

ISBN 978-88-55210-03-4

In thanking Maggie's for all the support they have
given us in building this new type of architectural
guide, we would like to highlight the great step that the
organisation has taken, after over 25 years of activity,
in opening its doors to the general public. "I suppose
people experience architecture in institutional settings
like large cathedrals, temples or other, whereas most
of us don't have access to great architecture in our
daily lives. That is what is wonderful about Maggie's,
that is open."
(From a conversation with Laura Lee and Marcia
Blakenham, London, May 2019).

Table of contents

Guidebook as a tool

This guide traces the history of Maggie's centres and outlines how they developed in Great Britain and elsewhere to become a new type of institution, a paradigm for architecture.

Founded by Maggie Keswick Jencks and Charles Jencks, both landscape designers, Maggie's centres offer psychological and practical support for people with cancer and their family and friends. Each centre is a 'hybrid' of four building types: "it is like a house which is not a home, a collective hospital which is not an institution, a church which is not religious, and an art gallery which is not a museum" (Jencks 2015).

When they are asked to design a centre, Maggie's architects are given the Architectural Brief, which is not a list of technical requirements but a description of the emotional and sensory states that the building should evoke or allow. "The buildings are and should all be of great visual impact due to their sophisticated architectural design, but at the same time be familiar with their domestic and welcoming spaces and be able to encourage people to support each other" (Jencks 2018).

Born as "Maggie's Cancer Caring Centre", over time the organisation has abandoned first "Cancer Caring" and then "Centre" to become "Maggie's Centre" and, more recently, only "Maggie's". However, in this volume, which focuses primarily on architecture, we will continue to call the building "Maggie's centre", but we will do so using the word "centre" with a lowercase "c" to help the organisation define itself simply as "Maggie's".

Maggie's centres

Laura Andreini*

While continuing to place the architecture-loving traveller at the centre of its attention and services, the On the Road series casts its gaze towards new horizons.

This book does not suggest itineraries to discover the contemporary side of a city. Instead, it proposes visits – as it is a tall order to combine them all in a single journey – to an extremely contemporary type of building. Or maybe one could say, it introduces the reader to a different way of devising and making architecture.

Maggie's centres are places whose mission is to help people with cancer. The idea came about thanks to the empathy of Maggie Keswick and her husband, architecture critic Charles Jencks. Maggie Keswick Jencks fell ill with cancer and during the course of her illness she realised that some aspects of the hospital environment could be off-putting for patients who not only needed treatment, but also "emotionally healthy" surroundings.

The idea, also thanks to the aid of famous architects, proved to be a great success. Now, over 25 years after the first centre was built, there are 28 Maggie's centres with many more currently under construction or in the planning phase.

When leafing through this book, readers/visitors will soon realise the immense contribution given by contemporary architecture in making a new category of outstanding buildings not only due to their type but also their therapeutic power. In addition, they provided the architects involved with an interesting design exercise. So, another piece is added to the puzzle of city guides, further underlining the direction taken by the series: travelling is not just ticking off places and experiences, but gaining new awareness and increasing our empathy.

* Laura Andreini is an architect and associate professor at DIDA, University of Florence. Co-founder of Studio Archea where she still works, she is also a writer and deputy editor for *area* magazine.

Exercises in style

Laura Andreini

A matter often at the centre of the architectural debate is whether a building – in general the building in question is a museum – should be a simple container or become an attraction, a work of art in itself. A question asked less often is if buildings are just "fences" around the actions of human life or if they can actually play a leading role in them. Can a building be as important as the actions that take place in it, by stimulating, avoiding or creating them?

Maggie Keswick Jencks's intuition, stemming from her dramatic personal experience, and her determination received support from her husband Charles and her nurse Laura Lee, today Maggie's CEO. As a result, they added a missing piece to the contemporary architecture scene. I am not just talking about the spread of a class of buildings that do not fit into the categories usually studied in universities, but the designer's actual *modus operandi* and their moral obligation to create architecture revolving 100 per cent around its users. There is not really anything new here. Architecture has played a salvific role in the past. The ancient Greeks sought catharsis by constructing buildings connected to landscapes modelled for the community's well-being. However, over the centuries, in particular the last two, this goal has faded in favour of efficiency. Buildings have to be built and used efficiently. Hospitals are a clear example of this: on one hand, these buildings are designed to make it easier to save our lives; on the other hand, however, little thought goes into the psychological effects that these places can have on patients shut up in a room for days on end, awaiting at times dramatic verdicts, or sitting in waiting rooms where their eyes rove around, unsuccessfully looking for something or somewhere to fix their sights on and dampen their anxiety.

Maggie's centres are a step towards filling the void in the vast scenario of contemporary design, created by architecture's increasing insensitivity towards the sensorial experience it is capable of providing. The result: standardisation nearly across the board. Buildings have the power to communicate and talk to us about sensations as well as functions. Many factors enable a person to "feel at ease" in a place: the presence of people, the reason for them being there, but also the scene that greets them, the harmony, materials, colours, lights and objects.

Maggie Keswick Jencks was aware of the need for a "beautiful" place where people could come to terms with even the worst news, where they could get to know and understand the illness whether alongside people who were having the same experience, or in solitude. It proved to be a winning idea: quite unexpectedly, the first centre was followed by many more, mainly located in the UK. Indeed, there are so many of them that we have even been able to create this architectural guide. Maggie's brainchild was followed by another one: the decision to allot each design to a different renowned architect, helping to attract attention to the charity organisation's mission.

Making this book brought to mind the brilliant work by Raymond Queneau, *Exercises in Style*, in which he repeats the same short story over and over using different styles, expressive techniques and grammatical rules. For Maggie's centres, the process is more or less the same. The story is the same, as are the functions and goals, but the end product is different every time depending on the context, the designer (unlike Queneau's exercises in style, which are all penned by the same writer), and the few rules to follow.

The upshot is that the architects involved in designing Maggie's centres have given birth to some true little masterpieces. Their exercise in style is no folly, no whim. It is bound to the lives of the people who will experience these spaces. All of these designs are the manifestation of the designer's will to produce the best because it is for a good cause. This, and the fact that they are free to move as they wish, with just a few, clear goals, sparks a creative process that sets the head spinning.

The result is different languages joined by three fundamental elements: light, freedom and beauty. Light takes centre stage in this architecture: it warms the space, instils a sense of calm and keeps people with cancer part of the living and beautiful world outside.

Maggie's serves a whole host of uses. You can breathe in the freedom. People with cancer can choose whether to deal with the tricky emotions they have to face alone or in a group, with a cup of tea or a book, or in a group therapy session where they can talk about their problems.

Centre users live in a place that is tailormade for their well-being. That is where the beauty of these centres lies. Every piece of furniture, every object, down to the mugs and glasses, has been chosen to make the people coming here feel at ease. It gives a home-from-home feeling, even though they know that is not where they are. Well-being is beauty.

Maggie's tackles a dramatic topic, they have a difficult goal. Nevertheless, Maggie and Charles Jencks's idea finds an original and fresh place in the panorama of contemporary architecture. In the freedom to express their creativity, the architects are conscious of the power that beautiful architecture has over people's well-being. Furthermore, the variety of solutions does not detract from the goal but becomes a real part of the Maggie's centre concept. This "little" exercise in style makes an enthusiastic foray onto the contemporary architecture scene and suggests a whole new way of putting buildings back on centre stage.

Maggie's architectural guide

Laura Lee*

This guidebook invites you to visit Maggie's, a network of over 25 cancer care centres with a unique architectural interest.

We are very lucky that some of the world's most renowned architects have designed a centre for us, many of them close friends of our founder Maggie Keswick Jencks and her husband, the architecture theorist Charles Jencks. Our brief is simple. Design a building that will help people with cancer feel better. Our landscapes are created by equally prominent designers who understand just how important gardens are in lifting your spirits. I hope you will agree that our centres and their gardens are unique, beautiful, and very special places.

Each Maggie's centre is different but you will see that most are small buildings in the grounds of large hospitals. As you approach a centre, the path and the planting should draw you towards the building – they should begin to instil a sense of calm. Once inside the centre, it should feel like a home, not a clinical place. There is no reception desk, and there are no signs on the doors. Maggie's expert staff don't have name tags – the idea is that people get to know them and remember their names.

The kitchen table is at the centre of each Maggie's. This is where people can start to talk to others who are in the same boat as them, have a cup of tea, talk to us, or just read or have a breathing space. You will see that there is plenty of light, lots of natural materials, and that every item, from furniture to crockery, has been chosen with care to create a space that feels familiar.

You'll find large, flexible rooms that can host a group session or a yoga class. There will be small, more private spaces where people can sit and think or have a rest after treatment. You will notice that each room is calm and safe, with inviting seating and warm blankets. Look out for views of trees and courtyard gardens, or even a tree in the middle of a building. Look up and you might see the sky above you. You will have forgotten that you are on a hospital site.

This book proposes a number of itineraries that will allow you to see several Maggie's centres in a day, depending on how you are getting around. You'll need to allow two or three days to do some of the routes. Our centres are open Monday to Friday 9 am - 5 pm, and our staff will be happy to show you around as long as they aren't busy with centre visitors.

You are so welcome, but when you visit please remember that these are working buildings and respect the privacy of our visitors, many of whom will be going through a difficult time. Please ask before taking photos.

I hope that you will enjoy visiting our centres and will see what a difference our programme of support and our beautiful buildings make for our visitors.

* Laura Lee, who was Maggie Keswick's nurse, has been Maggie's CEO since 1996. She was made Dame in the Queen's Birthday Honours list for her work in ensuring people with cancer the emotional support they need during their medical journey.

Map of Maggie's centres

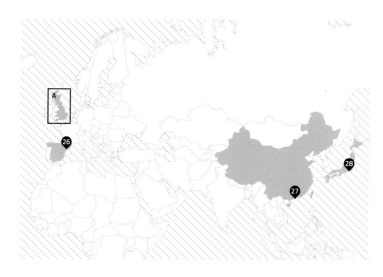

Countries
United Kingdom, Spain,
China, Japan

Website
www.maggies.org

Telephone
0300 123 1801

UK centres

01. Maggie's Edinburgh
02. Maggie's Fife
03. Maggie's Dundee
04. Maggie's Aberdeen
05. Maggie's Highlands
06. Maggie's Forth Valley
07. Maggie's Lanarkshire
08. Maggie's Glasgow Office
09. Maggie's Glasgow
10. Maggie's Newcastle
11. Maggie's Yorkshire
12. Maggie's Oldham

13. Maggie's Manchester
14. Maggie's Nottingham
17. Maggie's Oxford
18. Maggie's Cheltenham
19. Maggie's Swansea
20. Maggie's Cardiff
21. Maggie's Southampton
22. Maggie's at
The Royal Marsden
23. Maggie's West London
24. Maggie's Barts – London
(City & East)

Centres in development

15. Maggie's Coventry
16. Maggie's Northampton
25. Maggie's at The Royal Free

International centres

26. Kálida Barcelona
27. Maggie's Hong Kong
28. Maggie's Tokyo

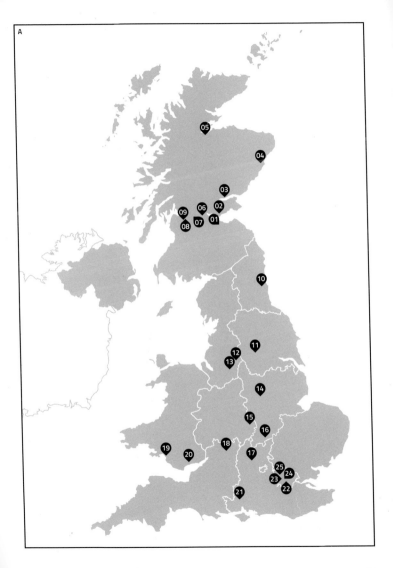

The sensory architecture of the Maggie's centre

Caterina Frisone*

In remembering Charles Jencks, to whom this small volume is dedicated, I wish to introduce the Maggie's centre and its philosophy to architects and non-architects alike, encouraging them to visit and experience its many centres. Founded in Edinburgh in 1996 by Maggie and Charles Jencks with the intent of bringing a new contribution to the construction of health, Maggie's is an open, free, non-clinical charity that provides practical and psychological support to people with cancer, their families, and their friends, all indistinctively called "visitors". Always built alongside the hospital, Maggie's centres stand out for their sophisticated architectural design which has proven to be a key component of their success. This environment is special in that it acts on the body and mind, contributing to a sense of well-being in people through stimulation of the senses. We know that what we see, smell, touch, or feel with our body influences our mental state, and the impressions we receive from the space around us impact our way of being. Architecture is an art that has the power to arouse emotions. Through space, material and light, it affects our conditions of calm, tension, self-confidence; in short, it has a psychological consequence for us.[1]

The sensory experience of architecture, combined with the therapeutic effects of nature, is not new. For more than eight centuries, the ancient Greeks offered healthcare, combining architecture and nature, placing magnificent buildings in beautiful settings rich in vegetation and spectacular views. In order to honour the healing god Asclepius, they built several healing centres, among which that of Epidaurus (V B.C.–IV A.D.) was the most celebrated healing centre in the classical world, and a notable example of holistic healthcare. The complex of the sanctuary buildings consisted of the *Asklepion*, the healing temple dedicated to God and around, the sacred *àbaton* or restricted dormitory for the sick who were ill and the *katagòghion* where the family members were welcomed to stay. Next to it were the gym, the stadium, the shared baths, and the theatre, used for recreation and leisure where the sick moved in harmony with doctors and priests. This fact, that is, the total integration between patients and staff, in the institutions that offer health services today, it never occurs and is what distinguishes Maggie's from all other organisations. As in ancient Greece, Maggie's, which still considers the mind as important as the body, offers an open and integrated model where staff and visitors share a sophisticated built environment that, in synergy with its psychological support programme, helps people with cancer to accept the disease, something that was unthinkable before. This flexible state of mind that is enabled in a Maggie's centre is embodied in the quote by Maggie Keswick Jencks: "Above all what matters is not to lose the joy of living in the fear of dying".

But who were Maggie and Charles Jencks? Maggie was a fashion designer, and she had also studied Chinese gardens. Her husband Charles was theorist and critic of architecture and created gardens and parks as a landscape

* Caterina Frisone is an architect, educator and researcher interested in the experiential side of architecture. Through her PhD thesis on the Maggie's centre she was able to assess how design can improve people's health and well-being.

1. From a coversation with Chris McVoy (Steven Holl Architects), May 2018

architect. They met in London in the 1970s at the AA, the Architectural Association, when she was a student and he was a lecturer. Since then, they have spent their time travelling, researching, and designing, which they continued to do later with their two children, Lily and John. In 1988, Maggie was diagnosed with breast cancer. After dealing with treatment and struggle, Maggie thought that she had recovered, until 1993, when the cancer returned, this time widespread. After waiting in "this awful interior space with neon lights and sad people sitting exhausted on these chairs", she was told the bad news: that she had two to three months to live. Then, the nurse came up and said: "I'm very sorry dear, but we'll have to move you out into the corridor, we have so many people waiting". After a short period of feeling dejected, Maggie decided to react and spend the remaining time designing an ideal place to help cancer patients. Together with her nurse, Laura Lee, visited the Wellness Foundation hospice in California to gather information and gain a better understanding about this type of facilities, where patients are encouraged to have a healthy diet and an exercise regime while staying in a pleasant environment. Returning to Edinburgh, Maggie convinced the doctors to support her idea, and in the end the hospital gave her an abandoned stable to be turned into her CCC, Cancer Care Centre. After interviewing four architectural firms, Maggie and Charles chose the Scottish architect Richard Murphy, who eventually adapted the small building so that it could house the activities that Maggie would have liked to offer to people with cancer. What was absolutely clear from the outset was the fact that the centre had to be complementary to the hospital, but not institutional: no corridors, signs, or information desks. If the centre doesn't look like a hospital, Charles wondered, then what is it? The answer was that it had to be like a house, where the kitchen was to be the core for socialising around a big table over a cup of tea. Starting from the design idea of a double-height space with a single entrance and four rooms, Murphy placed the kitchen and the sitting room suitable for hosting various activities on the ground floor, and two consultation rooms on the first floor. An aquarium was set in the centre of the library-stairs, as Maggie had requested. With the exception of the toilet, which was completely closed to allow people to cry without making themselves heard, in the centre there were no doors but sliding panels instead, so that the space could be split up into rooms or opened, with absolute flexibility. Outside, a rose garden was to be the horizon that Maggie would have enjoyed watching "amid attacks of harmful therapies". Thanks to her determination to complete the project, as well as some new and alternative therapies that she tried, Maggie survived another eighteen months, saying that her last year was "the best year of my life".

Maggie Keswick Jencks died in 1995 with the project drawings on her bed. The Edinburgh centre opened in 1996 and, although at the time there was no formal document, Maggie's wishes and ideas were soon collated in what was to become the Architectural Brief, the essence of Maggie's philosophy. With no expectation that there would be more than one centre, the Maggie's project began to grow. Between 2001 and 2005, Murphy doubled the size of Maggie's Edinburgh with two expansions, and three more centres were opened, in Glasgow (2002), Dundee (2003), and Highlands (2005). While Maggie's Glasgow The Gatehouse (today, Maggie's Office for Scotland) was another conversion of an existing building, the Maggie's centre designed by Frank Gehry in Dundee was a new construction that became a milestone in the history of the charity. Larger and with a greater visual impact, but still domestic, the white volume with its aluminum roof was the first building to be built in Great Britain by Frank Gehry. This drew the media, who started talking about the psychological impact that high-quality architecture has on people with cancer. After Gehry, several other world-renowned architects were invited to design a Maggie's centre, including Zaha Hadid with Maggie's Fife (2006) and Ivan Harbour and Richard Rogers (Rogers Stirk Harbour + Partners) with Maggie's West London (2008). Since 2009, the growth has been exponential, and Charles Jencks, Laura Lee and Maggie's best friend Marcia Blakenham have been instrumental in having more Maggie's centres built at even more hospitals, always using the same model of a small structure with an unconventional design. Today, there are a total of 28 Maggie's centres, many of which have received important architecture awards. In addition to the existing centres, several others are being built and designed and more and more hospitals are requesting to have one, as more and more architects offer to design new ones.

The most obvious feature of these buildings is that they are all different from each other. This variety arises from the Architectural Brief, the programme of the building given to architects when they are commissioned to design their own centre. Only a few pages long, the Brief does not prescribe technical solutions, but rather asks for spaces that would allow centre users to experience a variety of emotions, leaving the designers free to come up with their own interpretation. Although different in shape and location, the customised architectural solutions all communicate the same feelings. Since we cannot predict how people feel, especially when they have a serious illness, the space must be open and flexible to continuously change. In response to the Brief, the architects therefore provide a "menu" of spaces accessible to all, a shell that allows people to feel a range of emotions.[2] And, going beyond the Brief, the architects adopt a sensory design that affects body and brain through space, light, and materials. The sequence of spaces is divided or joined flexibly by sliding or revolving doors. In the continuity of spaces, which is also continuity of light, the spatial experience is that of an evolving space: large openings allow long perspectives on the horizon, transmitting feelings of control and safety; movable ceilings, coloured skylights and

2. From a conversation with Ellen von Loon (OMA), May 2018

large lanterns gives sensations of movement and action.[3] The forces that are created in these experiential fields are able to move people within the centre, making them feel wholly individual emotions. As many visitors describe it, it is the aura that stimulates the senses. In addition to the open space, in fact, it is the scenography made of bright colours, soft chairs, good smells – so different from those in the hospital – and the slow movement of people who walk quietly and speak calmly, that together contribute to a sense of physical comfort and generate states of mental well-being that are sometimes difficult to describe. Within this sensory environment, art works and design objects play an important role in focusing the mind on beauty, which is crucially important for people according to Maggie's psychologists. As the staff say, wherever they look visitors will always find something beautiful that will give them pleasure, and this helps them open up even in difficult conversations. The building is therefore not a simple container, but an indispensable member of the team; it is reassuring and "hugging". Whether talking to the centre staff or sitting alone, people will feel the contribution the building makes to their psychological well-being.

The physical space is as flexible as the support programme offered by Maggie's. There is no need to register and centre visitors are free to participate in any activity they choose. Furthermore, they are invited to feel no longer patient but people. To this end, people are encouraged to access any part of the building, as well as to help themselves making their own cup of tea like they would do at home, so that they feel it a "home from home". Everyone is free to use Maggie's as they wish, which emphasises its hybrid nature. "Indeed, a Maggie's centre is a hybrid of four types of buildings: a house which is not a home, a collective hospital which is not an institution, a church which is not religious, and an art gallery which is not a museum. But it has aspects or traces of these four types of buildings, used in a new way" (Jencks 2015).

This small building that in front of a hospital has the strength of David against Goliath, has managed to influence the architects first, then their other projects which in turn influenced other clients, as well as the users of the centres and the hospitals themselves. In short, Maggie's original idea for a small centre, a seed planted over 25 years ago, has generated a remarkably influential model that could become a paradigm for the design of other healthcare buildings and, perhaps, other building types.[4] Unlike the hospital, Maggie's communicates joy and energy, and this is its strength. The dream of Charles Jencks was to extend its model to other healthcare facilities for chronic diseases while that of Laura Lee is that the Maggie's centre, like healing temples in Greece, proliferate and reach every cancer hospital in Great Britain and elsewhere in the world. I am not sure this will happen, but what may happen is that, in the future, hospitals will stand out for having their own Maggie's centre.

3. From a conversation with Ivan Harbour (Rogers Stirk Harbour + Partners), July 2018

4. From a conversation with David Page (Page\Park), October 2018

Maggie's centres in context

Edwin Heathcote*

Where we were once born, gave birth, got ill and died in our homes now these landmark events take place in the hospital. Yet curiously there has been a reversal in the status and symbolism of the hospital and the buildings concerned with health, one which has taken them from esteemed components of culture, rich in art, to one which is an institution designed for machinery, efficiency, servicing, and car parking.

It wasn't always like this. For the Greeks the theatre was a healing building, a place in which architecture, nature, landscape, drama, and crowds together built a place of community catharsis. The writings of Vitruvius tell us that in Rome health was central to the understanding of architecture, percolating through every aspect, from orientation to ventilation. For the people of the Middle Ages there were abbeys and almshouses, hospitals executed in a refined Gothic style and hung with fine paintings and tapestries. In the seventeenth century hospitals in London and Paris became prestige projects, their domes symbols of the civilised city. In the Victorian era, with the burgeoning knowledge of infection and contagion, there was a revolution in hospital design; well-ventilated 'pavilion' blocks departed from each other and connected with elegant arcades.

And then, at the dawn of modernism, the idea of health and hygiene found itself at the heart of the modernist project. White buildings, naturally-lit with terraces for fresh air, featuring white-tiled interiors and linoleum floors. Josef Hoffmann, Alvar Aalto, Berthold Lubetkin and others created sanatoriums and health centres steeped in the new ideas of hygiene and efficiency. But those models were degraded over the twentieth century. Just as corporate banality, capital and commerce captured modernism and turned it into just another applied style, medical architecture was made global and generic, ignoring the lessons of millennia of civilisation in the name of efficiency. None of this is to say, of course, that the modern medical building is not a remarkable product of civilisation. Quite the opposite. The extraordinary procedures, interventions, and treatments that take place in these buildings are, arguably, a high point of our culture, but they are now taken for granted and their architecture has become bureaucratic and invisible.

What has been underserved in modern buildings for health is the soul. The idea that architecture could be something more than an armature for the processes and mechanics of healthcare. The Maggie's centres act as a health supplement for the hospital. They are not medical buildings in themselves but rather venues where the mind and body can be cultivated, where humanity can be a little restored, and where ailing and anxious bodies can find some respite in an expectation that architecture should provoke, challenge, excite, and perhaps relax.

The idea behind the buildings is that architecture has a role in supporting an enriched idea of life as something more than the physical accommodation

* Edwin Heathcote is an architect and architecture critic. With Charles Jencks, in 2010, he was the author of *The Architecture of Hope: Maggie's Cancer Caring Centres*. He is editor-in-chief of the online design writing archive readingdesign.org.

of the body and its treatment. Architects have worked to create buildings that are unexpected and different, each tailored to an idea of a holistic place in which a garden or a ray of sun, the smooth wooden surface of a dining table or a quiet corner with a view of a tree can help somewhat to restore life. It is a unique typology that sits between more established places, what Charles Jencks referred to as a hybrid of church, home, gallery, and community centre.

From the first designs for Edinburgh by Richard Murphy, through Frank Gehry's remarkable centre in Dundee, and on through Steven Holl's design for St Bartholomew's in London, the ideas have remained the same: a building that somehow blends domesticity, privacy, and community, one that acknowledges nature and accepts the artifice of architecture.

Some centres, like Zaha Hadid's crystalline design for Fife, and Rem Koolhaas's glass doughnut for Glasgow, seem counter-intuitive, as if they might be something far-removed from the cosy domesticity needed for an architecture of well-being. Yet they work, and work incredibly well, a radical, provocative architecture usually reserved for a global circuit of museums presented to the public as a gift. Buildings like Holl's at St Bart's take up a conversation with historic neighbours, while others, like Dow Jones's Cardiff centre, conjure a rich architecture from apparently austere means. Maggie's centres have grown into arguably the world's most compelling architecture programme, building a legacy of works by some of the greatest names in global design. They represent a way of distributing the intelligence and iconography of great architecture more evenly, and to those most in need of uplift and solace through space. It is a new typology, a hybrid idea that embraces complexity and expression, nature and art, and that, perhaps, points the way to an architecture of humanity.

Maggie's centres in hospital settings

Niall McLaughlin*

On a cold February day, the tiniest drop in temperature would have turned the steady rain to sleet or snow. The Scottish winter had leached the last colour from the landscape. I stood looking out across a car park from the empty reception area of the Beatson Cancer Centre in Glasgow. I was searching for signs to direct me to the Maggie's building. Outside the door, I saw nothing much except teeming wet tarmac gridded with windscreens and, beyond, on top of a slope, the gaunt ruin of a nineteenth-century asylum.

I was trying to imagine how I would feel if I had just received bad news from a doctor. Often, specialists are too busy to offer the kind of emotional help required and they can only send their distraught patients back out into corridors lined with plastic chairs. It helps to be able to hand out a leaflet directing patients to the Maggie's centre nearby. It might seem small, but it gives you something to do next.

As I stood on the narrow pavement, I became aware of the sheer banality and abstraction of my surroundings. There were signs with arrows pointing in every direction: names of buildings, instructions, warnings, and slogans. Chimneys, canopies, lamp-posts, litter bins, painted barriers, vans, and shrubs lay dotted around in no apparent order. Underneath it all, the tarmac was a scrambled tracery of white and yellow painted lines. The morning light was tinged with cold fluorescent hues from the looming hospital building. It was a perfectly ordinary place, known to all of us, lacking any vestige of comfort.

Then, on a hill at the edge of the scene, I saw a single light. It was a pendant lamp with a warm tungsten glow. I instinctively knew it was hanging above a dining table in a warm interior. It came from a building wreathed in trees and I guessed at once that this was where I was going. This tiny fragment in a confusing field of signs was enough to conjure an entire alternative world.

I made my way up a path to the building and I saw a colourful stack of information leaflets at the entrance. It was an invitation to pop in and pick one up. Within half a minute a man came over and asked me if I'd like a cup of tea. Make no mistake, tea is the fuel that powers the whole Maggie's project. I quickly found myself in conversation around the table beneath the golden lamp that I had seen calling me across the car park.

I spent a day there in the Maggie's centre. I met cancer specialists, psychologists, and a benefits advisor. I spoke to people who were dropping in for comfort, for practical advice, to take mindfulness classes, to reconnect with weekly support groups or to access benefits. The building was alive with small groups of folk chatting. Individuals read or reflected in quiet corners. People told me about their diagnoses, their experience of the disease and their prognoses. The atmosphere was open and it felt like a place where everyone could speak plainly about themselves. They could listen and be listened to. Cancer is a malady that we push away to the side of our lives if possible. In this building, people met it face to face together. Just being in the company of other

* Niall McLaughlin has been a London-based architect since 1991. His work was shortlisted for the Stirling Prize in 2013, 2015, and 2018 and exhibited at the Venice Architecture Biennale in 2016 and 2018. He is currently designing Maggie's Cambridge.

people living with cancer gave everyone strength. I was barely aware of the distinction between professional staff and visitors. It appeared that everyone was taking care of each other.

Architecture begins in community. A space is made by people for themselves and it can sometimes be framed by a building. Buildings are not agents in creating communities but they have a role to play. The Glasgow Maggie's centre I visited was un-showy, without any conscious virtuosity. It felt like an informal mid-century modern house. The architect was confident enough to leave a lot to the furniture and the landscaping. It was filled with lovely objects and paintings in a variety of settings, all beautifully linked. The gardens glowed, even on this gloomy day. What was important in this place was that the building and the community had been brought together in a way that contrasted with the other place across the car park. It created a completely different world.

The British National Health Service is a significant achievement of modern civilisation. It provides free at source healthcare to every citizen in the country. Despite its inefficiencies, it is a miracle of mass organisation and provision. It belongs to that group of entities created by social modernism that facilitate undreamed of possibilities at low cost for everyone. Supermarkets, air travel, universal education and free healthcare are all enabled by our collective ability to create highly efficient, large organisations. They have transformed the possibilities available to us, but they do so at the cost of abstraction and deracination in our ordinary experience. They produce places like orbital motorways, airports, and hospitals that we pass through in a blur in order to get back to the grounded parts of our lives. We accept the banal weirdness of these settings for what we get in return: long life, exotic foods, and guaranteed sunshine. Abstraction and extended experience are necessarily intertwined.

Hospitals have a history of prioritising high levels of organisation and efficiency over place-making and human experience. The stakes are high. Issues of hygiene and consistent process are properly prioritised and have to be achieved at low cost. Simple failings can have catastrophic results. Most hospitals are conceived as highly-tuned instruments designed to process the maximum number of people as efficiently as possible. The colossal cost of building them, with all its political implications, has driven health construction procurement to adopt abstract processes driven by risk management. If people can be considered as assemblages of mostly repairable components, hospitals are excellent workshops for mending them in quantity.

Healing, however, is a complex business with its own slow ways. Living well with incurable conditions is part of our whole-life experience. Sometimes we can't just pass through a hospital like an airport and we become entangled in its unhomely network. This is where other paradigms of health and living with illness have their place. It requires a community to carry the load. The quality of our experience and the interconnected needs of our predicament become a central concern. This is the place for a Maggie's centre in the context of our wider care for each other. Given the shared pact we all subscribe to, where good healthcare is free for all at an affordable tax point, it would be impossible – even undesirable – to set Maggie's centres as a universal aspiration for all hospitals. By getting the best architects to interact with talented nursing and counselling staff, and making beautiful, homely settings for reconciliation and healing, Maggie's have created refuges in the vast abstraction of modern hospitals. In doing so, they hold up a standard of care that challenges the wider organisation and spurs innovation in every part of the hospital. This is a highly productive discourse.

Later that same month, I visited the Maggie's centre in Oldham. It is a modern and light pavilion standing in front of the great hulk of the old hospital. You cross a little bridge into an airy wooden box. Immediately inside, there is a fluid glass wall enclosing a courtyard with one lovely tree. It was just coming into leaf with the first sense of spring. I chatted to a group of women who were part of a support group meeting in the building. I asked what they thought of the architecture and they all said that they loved it. "I'll tell you what it is", one of them said. "After I was diagnosed, I came in the door here and I saw that tree and I thought to myself, everything's going to be alright".

Maggie's centre gardens: herbs, habitat, and the search for deeper meaning

Lily Jencks*

The gardens at Maggie's centres are inalienable. That gardens themselves are therapeutic – and help with healing – is clear from both research and anecdote, but the gardens at Maggie's do more than that, by working at a number of levels to curate the care, content, and community that can make a huge difference to the experience of the centres' visitors. Gardens were central to the initial concept of Maggie's. When my mother, Maggie, published the first edition of *The Chinese Garden* in 1978, the first modern book on Chinese Gardens to be written by a Westerner, she discovered how these small gardens could represent the macrocosm of the world in the microcosm of the garden. This was achieved by Gongshi rocks representing the mountains in miniature, or the ponds' soft edges and corner-turning form representing the endless seas, and the planting framing space to imply the garden extends beyond the walls. To capture the panorama of the world in the miniature of a garden is to find a way to make a garden connect us to something larger than ourselves. At Maggie's that connection is fostered through a sense of community, through the way a garden encourages us to interact, and the several community gardening schemes. It is also present in the way a garden connects us to the rhythms and cycles of nature – in watching the flowering seasons, different birds or insects interacting in their habitats. Finally, the garden can be a place where the design can tell a story that metaphorically links to the larger narrative of the cancer-caring centres. In this short piece I want to investigate the various therapeutic uses of gardens for Maggie's centres, from the growing of herbs or collective gardening, to the creation of natural habitats for birds and butterflies; from the care of the natural environment, to symbolic qualities that can be meaningfully interpretated for visitors.

In *A View from the Front Line*, a short text that outlined her ideas for a new type of cancer care, my mother highlighted the qualities of the spaces in hospitals where cancer care is delivered. Talking of a comparison to the waiting rooms found in many hospitals she wanted to provide a better environment, stating:

'Waiting time could be used positively. Sitting in a pleasant, but by no means expensive room, with thoughtful lighting, a view out to trees, birds and sky, and chairs and sofas arranged in various groupings could be an opportunity for patients to relax and talk, away from home cares'.

Here her focus is on the view out, towards a natural setting, a feature in the oft-cited Roger Ulrich 1984 study[1] that linked patient post-operative recovery time in hospitals with views of natural landscapes. The access to a natural view, or even a route out of each room into the garden, is an important principle in the organisation of each of the Maggie's buildings. The buildings are usually porous to the garden, trying to bring as much of the natural setting into the centre, as least as much as is possible in our cooler climate. The plan of Rogers Stirk Harbour + Partners' centre at London's Charing Cross Hospital clearly demonstrates that building/garden hybrid. Within this building

* Lily Jencks is an award-winning architect who, inspired by her parents Maggie and Charles Jencks, integrates architecture, landscape and art. Her work ranges from urban parks to intimate interiors, creating green spaces derived from universal values.

1. Roger Ulrich, "View through a window may influence recovery from surgery", in *Science*, 224(4647), 1984, pp. 420-421

Dan Pearson planted three internal courtyards that puncture the building, each one with a specific plant combination to make the most of different views from each room. Each room has a different relationship with an external courtyard area, natural lighting, and the changing greens of the seasons.

The consultation rooms overlook a shared courtyard, and for the sake of privacy the windows are frosted, allowing the shadows of the magnolia trees to play against the glass. At the suggestion of a person with cancer, Pearson planted some peppermint and lemon verbena used for both tea and aromatherapy purposes. Although not a developed *hortus medicus* per se, the inclusion of an herb garden and medicinal botanical plants has been developed in several of Maggie's gardens, and able-bodied patients are encouraged to volunteer for garden maintenance, which provides both good exercise and therapeutic relief.

While the views from the rooms and towards the gardens are key design features for all Maggie's centres, the landscape that you travel through to access the buildings is also very important. This building is a 'bookend' to Charing Cross Hospital's prominent façade on Fulham Palace Road, one of the busiest bus routes in London. The building and landscape had to mitigate this aggressive urban environment, and each element, from the surrounding planting that brightly clashes with the optimistic-orange walls, and the internal courtyards, serve to turn the building away from the 1960s hospital tower and hustle of the street to a sanctuary of calm inside.

To enter Maggie's at Charing Cross, a woodland walk leads from the hospital gates to the door, between existing mature plane trees, under-planted with hardy decorative ground cover. This landscape is a buffer; a winding path providing a few moments of rest to shed the experience of the hospital you have just left. One of the hardest moments for patients and visitors is often the first visit to Maggie's. The first step through the threshold can be daunting, so an inviting pathway, with places to pause, offers an essential cushion to the process of entering and accepting help.

The second centre I would like to discuss is one that I myself worked on in Hong Kong as a landscape architect with the architect Frank Gehry. Like Maggie's West London, the plan is a 'wheel-spokes' organisation, with the central hub of the kitchen radiating out to the more private consultation rooms, library, and quiet room. Herbs are planted on the raised retaining wall, for use in the kitchen, and visitors are encouraged to engage with gentle gardening. In our design, we looked at the formal arrangements and spatial complexity of the Chinese Scholar's Gardens in New York, studying the use of water that continues around corners, the subdivision of spaces into smaller areas with framed windows, the soft planting, and the intense textures of paths, all of which serve to dissolve edges, and convince a visitor that the garden is larger than it really is. Without copying the language of the

Chinese Gardens, Maggie's Hong Kong works with similar principles to create spatial richness with a diversity of alcoves, nooks, and interior/exterior relationships. The resulting garden provides for both private moments and social gathering, to give people with cancer, family members, and consultants many options for different types of interactions. At Maggie's you are not behind the doctor's desk, but, rather, sitting on a terrace having tea with a therapist, or busy gardening as another patient walks past, admiring the early-flowering daffodils, opening up an opportunity for further exchange and connection. By changing the environmental context of the visitor, we hope to offer opportunities to change their thinking about cancer.

Maggie's Hong Kong sits nestled between two ponds. As you enter the building several views of the garden immediately pull you towards the natural light, while darker spaces recede into the private consultation rooms. Gehry wanted the consultation rooms to sit like Chinese 'rocks' in the garden, each individually connected to the main space, thus providing views towards the garden in every direction.

Anecdotally unpacking Ulrich's study, I have discussed with patients their relationships and use of Maggie's gardens; they are all helped by their green environment: for some it might be a connection with the changing seasons, and the fighting desire to live to see the next flush of bloom on a rose. For others, a diagnosis makes every sensuous experience more intense, so that a magnolia's perfume caught on the wind provides vivid delight, or a 'lambs-ear's' soft down feels particularly delicate, and the sunlight on a rock casts even deeper shadows. Meeting users of Maggie's provides ample evidence of the efficacy of the gardens to increase a sense of well-being and belonging in a sensuous world: the 'joy of life' is palpable.

Views out to a landscape were also a defining factor in the organisation of the third centre I will discuss, the one in Glasgow. This one was designed by the architect Rem Koolhaas, while the landscape was designed by me in collaboration with Harrison Stevens Landscape Architects. The building is organised as a series of rectangular rooms linked around a courtyard. The movement through the building brings you into different relationships with the garden with each rotation of the geometry, facing first the exterior landscape, and next the interior courtyard.

Similar to Maggie's West London, the surrounding landscape is an important buffer between the centre and the hospital campus. To emphasise this buffer, and create a sense of sequence as visitors arrive, there is a swale or planted ditch around the building that provides seasonal wetland planting, and creates a small bridge-effect at the entrance. This thin strip of wetland planting changes over the seasons, allowing different plants to grow, and offering an important habitat for the local birds and butterflies. While this relatively small project is a nod to the wider ecological aims of increased biodiversity, bringing a number of birds and butterflies closer to the centre delights the people with cancer. Continuing west of the building, there is a path that extends from the circulation and zigzags through the trees. At the end of this loop is an installation of stumps that were created from trees felled during construction. These stumps are cut to resemble an inverted dome, with mirrored surfaces on top of each stump to reflect the sky. This creates a calm space to sit, for a family group or for individual consultations. It is an outdoor 'room' sometimes used for yoga or Tai Chi. It is also a moment of surprise: to see sunlight on the woodland floor. These moments of surprise can be a welcome distraction from a visitor's potentially distressing state of mind, to remind visitors of the joy of experience, and pleasures away from disease.

The last Maggie's landscape I'd like to present was designed by my father Charles Jencks, whose major landscape works seek to connect visitors to the cosmological principles that comprise our universe. At Maggie's Highlands in Inverness, Charles Jencks worked in collaboration with the Scottish firm Page\Park. The landscape and building are conceptually and formally intertwined. The inspiration for the design comes from a diagram of cells dividing – mitosis.

Healthy cell division is the basis for all of life. Cancer comes from this same process, but it is out of control, with cells dividing so fast as to create tumours that spread throughout the body. Here the landscape and building together form a meaningful narrative that connects visitors not just to views of nature, but the biological forces that create nature as well, while also conveying meaning to Maggie's centres' specific programme. While the curving and folding forms used in the building create the sense of enclosure and embrace Maggie's programmatic needs, the additional layer of meaningful form may also offer the visitor a new way to think about her cancer, and the laws that create all life.

At Maggie's the environment around the patient is carefully considered and cared for. If we are to create a healing environment, it must be with ecological thinking regarding the individual with their caregivers, the building with the garden around it, the habitat that garden contains, and the health of the environment beyond. Gardens have a multifunctioning therapeutic capacity, both at the scale of the ecological functions – cleaning air, providing habitat, replenishing groundwater – as well as at the scale of the individual visitor – muffling noise, providing light exercise, delighting with smell, colour and touch. Coupled with these therapeutic functions the centres are also delightful and beautiful, appealing to the many aspects of a visitor's experience, not just their needs as people affected by a disease. The design of Maggie's communicates to the visitor that there is still dignity and pride to be found in living with cancer, thanks to the help of Maggie's centres.

UK Routes

A. Scotland
B. Northern England
C. The Midlands /
   Central England
D. Wales / South-western
   England
E. Greater London / Eastern
   England / Southern
   England

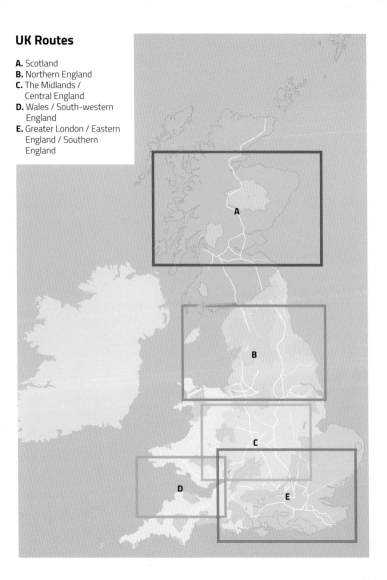

Itinerary A
Scotland

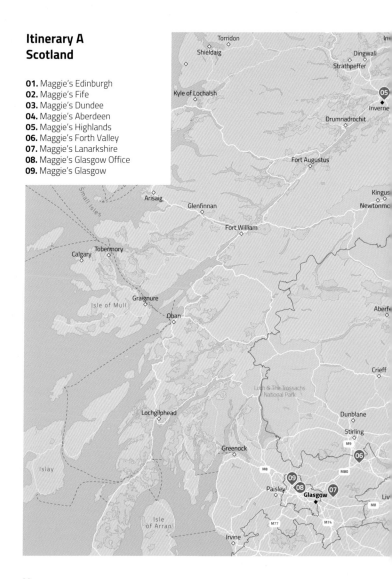

Lossiemouth
Forres   Elgin   Buckie
                              Banff   Fraserburgh
            Keith
Aberlour
    Dufftown
                                    Peterhead
                              Cruden Bay
                    Inverurie
Cairngorms
National Park   Ballater
                        Aberdeen   04
                        Stonehaven
            Forfar   Montrose
Blairgowrie
            Arbroath
    Dundee
    03
    Saint Andrews
Glenrothes
02
                North Berwick
01
Edinburgh   Dunbar
A68
                                A1

0   10   30 km

01. Maggie's Edinburgh

Western General Hospital
Crewe Road South,
Edinburgh EH4 2XU,
United Kingdom

Mon - Fri / 9 am - 5 pm

+44 131 537 3131
edinburgh@maggies.org
www.maggies.org

Located at the end of the hospital ground, opposite the Oncology Unit, the small, derelict stone building was magically transformed by Richard Murphy into the first Maggie's centre. Being one of the few converted from an existing building, since its opening in 1996 the centre has been expanded twice, more significantly in 2001 with the addition of the large sitting room and, more recently in 2018, with a new volume containing a group activity room that has created a new entrance courtyard. On the left side of the front door, the bronze bust of Maggie by Penelope Jencks welcomes the visitor.

Once inside, we will be warmly welcomed by a colourful double-height space characterised by yellow walls, green stairs and red steel structural profiles. Here, Murphy employs some clever tricks. By making the ceilings of the two floors deliberately very low and inserting a long skylight into the roof, he manages, on the one hand, to create a sense of intimacy and, on the other hand, to make the double-height space appear higher. To the right of the entrance we find the kitchen, the most important room in the centre, shielded from the outside by glass block walls. By placing the open kitchen near the front door and joining it to the open staircase, completely banishing corridors, Murphy establishes a spatial typology that would later become one of the central concepts of the Architectural Brief and a distinctive feature of future centres. Walking up the stairs incorporate a bookcase as well as

Maggie's Edinburgh, 1996
(extensions: 2001, 2018).
New entry courtyard, with
the original building in the
centre between the two
extensions

© Ben Black

architect
Richard Murphy OBE
of Richard Murphy Architects

landscape architect
Emma Keswick

construction
1995 - 1996
Extensions: 2001, 2018

→
The welcome area opens in the double-height colourful space with open kitchen below combined with the library-staircase and office above (top left); the group activity room features a central skylight and comfortable sofas in the space of the latest extension (top right)

↘
The large kitchen table is protected by the glass block wall between the kitchen and the entry courtyard

two seats and light wells inside small niches, where people can isolate, but still remain part of the scene. Upstairs, on the left, we find a consultation room and, on the right, the office. The first floor serves as a balcony overlooking the main entrance to join the two floors in a large open space.

Returning downstairs and proceeding to the right, at the end of the pink wall we find the sitting room. The large room can be split into one-third and two-thirds, making a smaller and a larger room when required. The mirrors positioned on the long skylight double the natural light and create the illusion of having ample space even when the dividing screens are closed. The skylight helps to let natural light into the space, whose luminescence in Scotland is six times greater when collected horizontally rather than vertically. Reinforcing the connection with nature, the large corner window widens to become a veranda, while on the opposite side, a new panorama opens up onto a natural woodland, with the main hospital building out of sight.

1. Entrance / Welcome area
2. Library
3. Kitchen
4. Consultation rooms
5. Group activity room
6. Large sitting room
7. Terrace

02. Maggie's Fife

Victoria Hospital
Hayfield Road,
Kirkcaldy KY2 5AH,
United Kingdom

Mon - Fri / 9 am - 5 pm

+44 1592 647997
fife@maggies.org
www.maggies.org

Boldly located on the edge of a hollow, between the hospital parking lot and the natural landscape, this sharp-edged geometrical building establishes a north-south directionality, having asphalt coated solid sides and transparent main elevations. Although the design intention was to let the visitor coming from the hospital enter the space from the north side, Maggie's Fife seems more inviting on the south side where the access via a ramp merges into a large terrace. Provocative yet powerful, the outdoor space defined by folded railings, concrete floor and wide roof overhangs find a welcoming dimension as soon as we glimpse inside. In contrast to the monolithic black volume, the bright and white interior space, opened and column-free along the glass façade, reveals another world. Pure spaces make us feel recharged, transferring energy and uplifting our spirit. We enter and as we walk, we notice that the inclined or curved walls, reinforced by horizontal shelves and invigorated by triangular cuts of light, move us into the dynamic space revealing its domestic dimension. The open kitchen at the heart generates a sequence of spaces around it: the office, the consultation rooms, the toilet, and finally, the library and the large sitting room or group activity room.

↗
Maggie's Fife, 2006.
The south façade of the enveloping building opens and extends into the landscape derived from the leftover hollow of a coal mine that was transformed into a wild garden

© Werner Huthmacher

architect
Dame Zaha Hadid
of Zaha Hadid Architects

landscape architect
Gross Max

construction
2005 - 2006

© Werner Huthmacher

1. Entrance / Welcome area
2. Office
3. Consultation rooms
4. Kitchen
5. Library
6. Large sitting room /
   Group activity room
7. Terrace

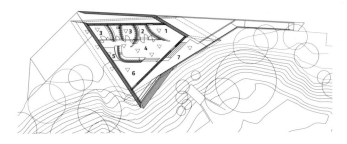

0 2 5m

© Chris Gascoine

© Chris Gascoine

↖
The geometric, sharp-edged, asphalt-clad building opens up to the hospital, inviting visitors to enter

↑ ↗ →
The library and kitchen areas are very bright thanks to their view of the garden (top left and right); and triangular cuts of light reveal the open, column-free space along the glass façade of the large sitting room (bottom)

03. Maggie's Dundee

Ninewells Hospital
Tom McDonald Avenue,
Dundee DD2 1NH,
United Kingdom

Mon - Fri / 9 am - 5 pm

+44 1382 632999
dundee@maggies.org
www.maggies.org

Being the first newly built centre, Maggie's Dundee attracted a lot of media attention when it was open in 2003, partly because this was Frank Gehry's first building in the UK, designed after the completion of the Guggenheim Museum in Bilbao. Having been close friend with Maggie and knowing what interested her, Gehry found inspiration in a lighthouse for the tower and in the pleated shawl of the woman from Vermeer's *Young Woman with a Water Pitcher* for the corrugated stainless-steel roof.

Located on the opposite side of the labyrinth designed by Arabella Lennox-Boyd, under the attentive gaze of Antony Gormley's sculpture *Another Time*, the white volume of Maggie's Dundee stands out on the grassy slope, with a nice façade that, appearing to almost smile, looks out onto the hospital. The entrance, as "obvious" as required by the Architectural Brief, practically draws the visitor into the building. Inside, the welcome area opens into a large space under a skylight and overlooks a long, narrow pier that projects into nature. The timber of the intricate structural ceiling that runs through the entire building releases a lively warm feeling, guiding the visitor through the space.

Perfectly balanced between open and closed plan, the space opens up allowing you to glimpse various rooms. The kitchen, separated by a glass door which is usually left open, is a large, homey space overlooking nature through full-height windows. Full of sunlight, it is always packed

↗
Maggie's Dundee, 2003.
Inspired by a lighthouse,
the building is located right
in front of the hospital on
a large lawn with dense
vegetation behind it

© Gehry Partners, LLP

© Gehry Partners, LLP

architect
Frank Gehry

landscape architect
Arabella Lennox-Boyd

construction
2002 - 2003

→
The kitchen is a large area with floor-to-ceiling windows

↘
The internal atmosphere is always very lively with guests and volunteers

with visitors and volunteers preparing food and drinks for anyone who comes in. Returning to the main entrance, on the righ-hand side, if we enter the toilet, we will find a frame with the stamps of Maggie's Dundee; next to it, the large sitting or group activity room, where Tai Chi and relaxation classes are held, is a welcoming space with a single window looking towards the sky. Inside the tower volume, from the library we access the first floor where a quiet space with a fireplace and a large tapestry by Eduardo Paolozzi opens onto the horizon. With a surprising view of the natural landscape and the River Tay, the consultation room acts as a great support during one-to-one sessions. This tower with a view is the lighthouse that Gehry dedicated to Maggie and all users of the centre. Along with many masterpieces of art and design, including Frank Gehry's *Wiggle Side Chair*, Maggie's Dundee features a beautiful rose garden, tended by the gardening group and where visitors practice yoga during the summer.

1. Entrance / Welcome area
2. Library
3. Office
4. Kitchen
5. Large sitting room / Group activity room
6. Consultation rooms
7. Terrace

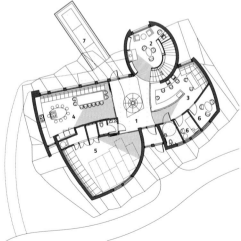

© Gehry Partners, LLP

04. Maggie's Aberdeen

Elizabeth Montgomerie Building, Aberdeen Royal Infirmary Hospital
Westburn Road,
Aberdeen AB25 2UZ,
United Kingdom

Mon - Fri / 9 am - 5 pm

+44 1224 645928
aberdeen@maggies.org
www.maggies.org

Like a pebble on the grass, Maggie's Aberdeen sits alone on the green lawn in front of the hospital. The distinct building is conceived as a pavilion in the park with a group of beech trees marking the main entrance and a row of cherry trees in the back. Revealing what is there and inviting us inside, large circular cuts sculpt the white shell in three moments: twice vertically, to shape the front entrance arch and the rear full-height window, and once horizontally to semi-cover the internal courtyard and allow visitors to be in contact with nature even when it rains.

After pausing in the entrance courtyard, we move inside through a small tunnel, finding an unexpected and friendly space. Our eyes are drawn towards the ceiling where colourful skylights radiate life energy, before looking around and noticing the *Pelican Chairs* that seem to say 'Welcome'. It is a space that conveys a calm atmosphere and sense of embrace, that is why they call this centre "hug". After taking a breath, we begin to explore the building, starting our sensory experience of this holistic space. Made of two components - the white concrete shell and the hardwood blocks containing the rooms - Maggie's Aberdeen invites us to use the space. Moving between the wooden volumes, on the ramp of the internal corridor, touching and feeling the warm timber, we move fluidly and harmoniously from a contained space to an open one, from looking up to now looking down. If we step into the wooden "boxes",

↗
Maggie's Aberdeen, 2013.
Sitting in front of the hospital,
surrounded by greenery,
the oval-shaped pavilion
envelops the centre while
the wooden boxes create
intimate rooms and spaces

© Snøhetta

architects
Snøhetta

landscape architects
Snøhetta

construction
2012 - 2013

→
The 360-degree open
entrance welcomes us
with coloured skylights
and enveloping *Pelican Chairs*

↘
The kitchen overlooks
the garden through a large
window with shelves of
aromatic herbs

here we find a library, there a staircase where
we can sit and enjoy the space, or further down
some niches, a fireplace, toilets and two consultation rooms where we can be alone or gather
as group when we feel more sociable.
While the timber blocks constitute a single unit
per se in the centre of the open plan, the two
long side walls are left free of furniture featuring only a single, long bench that incorporates
a gap of light, while resolving the connection
between curved wall and floor. On the kitchen
side, the bench stops in front of the large window. Shelves filled with teacups and pots of
herbs act as a screen on the window, protecting the privacy of people gathered around the
oval table from the world outside. The familiar,
domestic atmosphere is enriched by rugs (which
also help the acoustics), "huggable" furniture
and artworks by regional artists.

1. Entrance
2. Welcome area
3. Kitchen
4. Consultation rooms
5. Group activity room
6. Library
7. Large sitting room
8. Patio

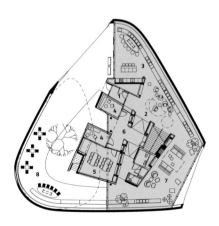

© Snøhetta

0   2   5 m

05. Maggie's Highlands

Raigmore Hospital
Old Perth Road,
Inverness IV2 3FL,
United Kingdom

Mon - Fri / 9 am - 5 pm

+44 1463 706306
highlands@maggies.org
www.maggies.org

On a site at the edge of Raigmore Hospital, Page\Park designed their building intertwined with Charles Jencks' landscape project. Inspired by the theme of cell division, the general plan provides for a flow of cells, two of which are single cells represented by two mounds, while two others are the result of the division of one cell into two (mitosis), an inverted mound (the building) and a void (the garden). Considering the garden as the starting point, Maggie's Highlands is a building that unifies spaces and joins to the landscape, in a continuous relationship with nature.

Entering the building from the hospital side through the square-frame door, we find ourselves in a space that is already an outward projection. Above us, the long horizontal skylight that runs along the building puts us in visual contact with the sky while revealing the spiral nature of the structure. From the entrance, with the kitchen on the left and the library on the right, we move into the "nucleus of the cell", an almond-shaped space surrounded by small, private consultation rooms and toilets. On the right, by moving sliding doors and walls, the large sitting room and library can become a single collective space.

While the tapering interior that swells upwards and the walls of the main space are leaning in different directions, the shape of the building ties in with that of the body: by widening at the shoulders and narrowing at the feet, we

↗
Maggie's Highlands, 2005. Intertwined with the landscape designed by Charles Jencks, the green building is a symbol of life. The inspiration for the design comes from a diagram of dividing cells, mitosis

architects
David Page and
Andy Bateman

landscape architect
Charles Jencks

construction
2004 - 2005

→
The kitchen area has a close connection with the sky thanks to the large skylight that illuminates all interior spaces

↘
By opening doors and sliding walls, the different social spaces can become a single collective space, joining the two living rooms and opening them to nature

embody the space. The physical relationship with the space that we inhabit influences our sensory experience while creating a sense of embrace and movement. The sensory experience is strengthened by the use of natural materials, too: as we walk up the stairs to the office, we can touch the curved beam cladded in timber and the solid birch plywood of the roof shell.

Integration between architecture and nature, enhanced by the green colour, symbol of life, is also evident in the proportions of the spaces and in the structural technology. With the metalwork developed at the same time as the geometry of the spirals, Page\Park managed to unify "structure", "function" and "beauty" of the building in a single movement: the geometry of the volume comes, surprisingly, from a single sheet, curved and inclined. Outside, Jencks' landscape with its paths and hillocks encourages movement and reminds visitors of the pleasure of being alive and invites them to enjoy nature, even by positioning sitting at the top of the mounds for a longer stay.

1. Entrance
2. Welcome area / Kitchen
3. Library
4. Consultation room
5. Office

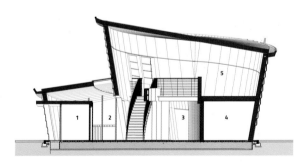

0   2   5 m

06. Maggie's Forth Valley

The Nina Barough Building
Forth Valley Royal Hospital,
Off Quintinshill Drive,
Larbert FK5 4SG,
United Kingdom

Mon - Fri / 9 am - 5 pm

+44 1324 868069
forthvalley@maggies.org
www.maggies.org

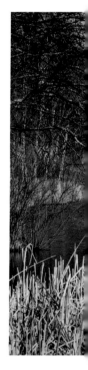

As it is some distance away from the hospital, you can use the car service from the hospital reception to reach Maggie's Forth Valley. Taking over the project from another architect during the construction phase, Garbers & James quickly managed to design a new building starting from the existing concrete slab. Although the three-winged scheme and external mass have remained, the project has been completely transformed through a geometry of straight lines that creates a sense of movement, which for Maggie's is fundamental. The inspiration for the new design came from the blurry natural colours typical of Scotland (purple, pink, orange, intense blue, with colours that we might see reflected on the scales of a fish) and the idea that, being on a lake shore, the building invokes a primordial return to nature. The pavilion could be seen as a bird-watching refuge or a fisherman's house, where people can walk barefoot on the warm, dry wooden floor, or take a rowing boat to go fishing.

From the outside, the colour of the materials helps the building blend in with the natural environment. Its mushroom-shaped canopies generate a sense of movement and protection and encourages us to enter. Once inside, the open space with bright colours, voices and good smells stimulates our senses of sight, hearing and smell making us feel a multisensory experience. In addition, the rhomboid-shaped skylights, which reflect the light of the sky with

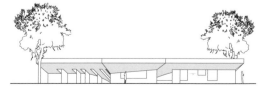

↗
Maggie's Forth Valley, 2017.
On the edge of a lake, the
pavilion induces a primordial
return to nature and invites
birdwatching or fishing

architects
Garbers & James

landscape architect
Darren Hawkes

construction
2015 - 2017

a system of backward mirror, create a kalei-
doscopic sensation. From the central space,
where the bright yellow kitchen counter and
the dry-assembled table act as the heart, the
centre extends towards the three arms of the
building. The space allows the user to choose
between various routes and to move easily,
avoiding busy areas that people can sometimes
find overwhelming.

The lake view is highlighted through the relationship between seats and windows, such as
the bench in front of the low arched window
with a view. For Maggie's, the act of sitting and
the chair as object are of primary importance. At
Maggie's Forth Valley, the fixed seats arranged
at the edge of the space of the large sitting
room to our right generate a sense of order
which, in turn, gives us calm and tranquillity.
At the same time, mobile furniture nurtures
variety and movement, also enhanced by their
warm colours and the colourful art is in continuous dialogue with the architecture.

1. Entrance / Welcome area
2. Kitchen
3. Computer desk
4. Large sitting room /
   Group activity room
5. Office
6. Consultation rooms
7. Library
8. Terrace

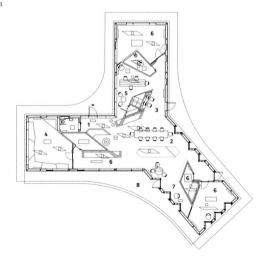

0   2   5 m

© Garbers & James

© Garbers & James

07. Maggie's Lanarkshire

The Elizabeth Montgomerie Building
Monklands Hospital,
Monkscourt Avenue,
Airdrie ML6 0JS,
United Kingdom

Mon - Fri / 9 am - 5 pm

+44 1236 771199
lanarkshire@maggies.org
www.maggies.org

On the site of the ancient Airdrie House, once protected by a belt of linden trees that survived the 1960s demolition, Maggie's Lanarkshire communicates a sense of being sheltered from the nearby hospital. The new garden is as poetic as it was in its original conception: a civilised place, a paradise.

The sequence inside the perforated brick wall is a seamless transition. From a quiet entrance courtyard animated by the sound of running water where we can pause, we enter a continuous domestic space interspersed with transparent light-filled enclosures. Thanks to a unique way of bringing light into the space of a little internal courtyard, a bit of Northern Light is caught at this latitude in the winter. The addition of a little sparkle completes Reiach and Hall Architects' intention to bring the sunlight down to the floor of the courtyards. The soft atmosphere generated by wood finishes in a variety of light woods gives the impression of a calm place, but soon we feel being moved on in space: the transparent perspective views, the linear rhythm of the ceiling structure and the horizontal shelves are catalysts of movement. Moving through the kitchen, living room and library, with glimpses of art, we find ourselves outside again, in the garden where old and new inhabitants – lime trees and Maggie's users – now live together in harmony and respect.

↗
Maggie's Lanarkshire,
2014.
The rear east façade
overlooks the new
walled garden

© David Grandorge

architects
Reiach and Hall Architects

landscape architects
rankinfraser

construction
2013 – 2014

1. Entrance courtyard
2. Welcome area
3. Office
4. Kitchen
5. Large sitting room /
   Group activity room
6. Library
7. Consultation rooms
8. Walled garden

0 2 5   10 m

←
The fireplace creates a
very peaceful atmosphere
contrasting with the feeling
of living in a dynamic space

→
The continuous space is
interspersed with wells of
light which, thanks to the
copper of their lantern, add
a little sparkle with the sun
and increase the sound of the
flowing water with the rain

↓
The light coming from the
large windows combined
with the rhythm of the ceiling
structure are catalysts of
simultaneous silence at the
kitchen table and movement
all around

© David Grandorge

© David Grandorge

08. Maggie's Glasgow Office

10 Dumbarton Road,
Glasgow G11 6PA,
United Kingdom

Mon - Fri / 9 am - 5 pm

+44 300 123 1801
enquiries@maggies.org

On the edge of Kelvingrove Park, converted from a Scottish baronial style lodge that used to be the gatehouse of a gigantic hospital, former Maggie's Glasgow The Gatehouse was replaced by the new Maggie's Glasgow (Gartnavel), following the demolition of the hospital. Although the external volume still seems to be part of the city, Page\Park's project only seeks contact with nature. The building now houses Maggie's office for Scotland, although when people visit and the kitchen is used, it still feels like a Maggie's centre.

Following Murphy's spatial model of the open-plan house at Maggie's Edinburgh, in the Page\Park's project the kitchen, placed near the entrance, is once again the starting point of the sequence of spaces and functions in continuous contact with nature. Moving up to the large sitting room, where flexible walls allow continuity of space, we will enjoy the landscape through the large gable window; climbing the spiral stairs to the upper floors, we can glimpse the sky through the tower skylight. The journey ends in the former consultation room; from here we can look out onto the garden with seats and the symbolic DNA sculpture designed by Charles Jencks, a place to contemplate the truths of nature: the beauties and struggles of life.

↗
Former Maggie's Glasgow
The Gatehouse, 2002.
The location of the building
next to Kelvingrove Park
places it in close relation
to the city

architects
David Page and Karen Nugent

landscape architect
Charles Jencks

construction
2001 - 2002

1. Entrance / Welcome area
2. Library
3. Kitchen
4. Consultation rooms
5. Sitting room / Fireplace
6. Large sitting room
7. Garden

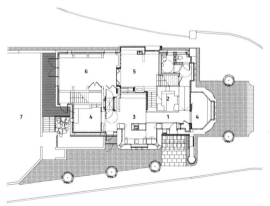

0   2   5 m

←
Exterior view from Kelvingrove Park. In the centre, the new steep gable window with wooden frame. On the right the DNA sculpture designed by Charles Jencks

↑
Although the building is not used as a centre, the kitchen space retains its family atmosphere

→
The sitting room opens up onto the landscape through the large window

09. Maggie's Glasgow

Gartnavel General Hospital
1053 Great Western Road,
Glasgow G12 0YN,
United Kingdom

Mon - Fri / 9 am - 5 pm

+44 141 357 2269
glasgow@maggies.org
www.maggies.org

Maggie's Glasgow sits on a gently sloping hill between the original Gothic Revival hospital building and the new Gartnavel General Hospital. By extending an existing wooded area over part of the hospital parking lot, OMA produced a flat-roofed, ring-shaped building completely surrounded by trees which block views of the hospital. The remarkable transformation of the site from "non-place" to "place" demonstrates the power that architecture has in bringing about change. Knowing also that nature plays a fundamental role in healing, OMA therefore chose that the garden had to be the most important "material" of the building. Enveloped by trees, OMA also imagined a poetic place for meditation where people can be alone or socialise, and Lily Jencks created a seating area outside with stumps of old trees topped with mirrors, representing calm and reflection. As soon as we arrive at the entrance, we are enticed to start walking, making a decision on which way to go: if we hear voices coming from the kitchen and are looking for company, we will go to the left, if we seek privacy, in a more peaceful environment, we will go right. Without realising it, the design of the ceiling in concrete and wood makes us move in space. To stimulate curiosity, OMA establishes a close relationship between design and landscape and creates a sequence of different types of spaces. Following the incline of the land, the communal spaces at the front of the building with panoramic

↗
Maggie's Glasgow, 2011. The ring-shaped building is completely surrounded by trees within a large green area

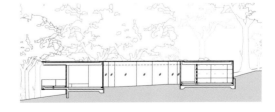

architects
Rem Koolhaas,
Ellen van Loon of OMA

landscape architect
Lily Jencks,
Harrison Stevens Landscape
Architects

construction
2010 - 2011

→ ↘
Shrouded in trees, the
outdoor seating area invites
us to meditate on ancient
tree stumps cut to resemble
an inverted dome

views onto the hospital increasingly give way,
as we enter the hill, to the private spaces of
the library, meditation room (the most private
space in the centre) and toilet, which used to be
called "private" as in the old days. The third type
of space is for "consultation" that with "social-
isation" and "privacy" constitute the three fundamental themes and purposes of Maggie's.
The centre is meant to feel like a home, with
the type of furniture we would find in a home:
a carpet, a lamp, an old sofa that helps create
the domestic atmosphere. Light, colour and art
create further sense of familiarity. The rooms
all have large sliding doors that can be opened
or closed, giving the space a double reading: a
sequence of social spaces or a building without a corridor, if the doors are open; a series
of private rooms with a corridor, if the doors
are closed. If only one door closes, the space
changes again, the corridor joins the courtyard to become a continuous space; however,
if it opens, we will feel part of the space of the
room and we will be drawn to the forest behind.

1. Entrance
2. Welcome area / Library
3. Kitchen
4. Office
5. Computer desk
6. Consultation rooms
7. Large sitting room /
   Group activity room
8. Garden

0 2   5 m

Itinerary B
Northern England

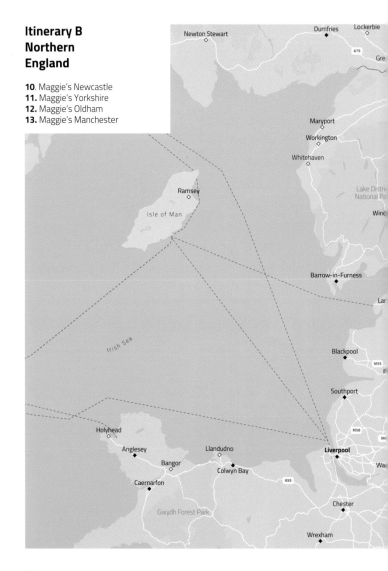

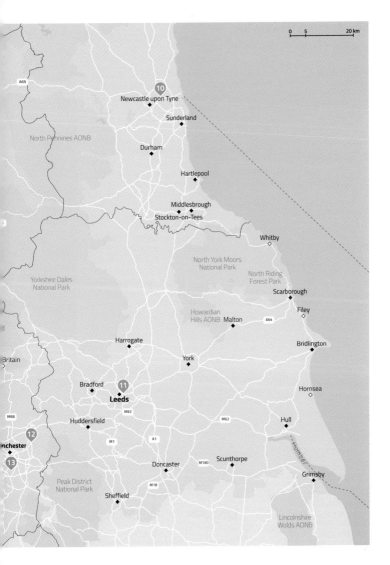

10. Maggie's Newcastle

Freeman Hospital
Melville Grove,
Newcastle upon Tyne NE7
7NU, United Kingdom

Mon - Fri / 9 am - 5 pm

+44 191 233 6600
newcastle@maggies.org
www.maggies.org

Located northwest of the hospital, Maggie's Newcastle was conceived as a creature emerging from the ground. Protected from its surroundings by artificial embankments, the L-shaped volume strengthens its relationship with nature, forming a peaceful courtyard of beeches, cherry trees, wild flowers, and aromatic herbs. With "concrete roots" reaching deep into the ground and using corten cladding indiscriminately for retaining walls and fronts, the complex building-landscape speaks the language of the earth and creates an engaging sensorial experience for its users. Highlighted by the drum above, the entrance invites us into this microcosm.

As soon as we enter, we are struck by the glow of the central space that combines beauty, structure and function. The orange bench acts as a base for the window frame which supports the inclined solar roof; the wooden staircase that doubles up as a bookshelf invites us to sit or continue towards the mezzanine and the roof terraces. With various uses and degree of comfort, the two wings of the building offer different spaces and light conditions. Known as a centre with a high male attendance, the shaded activity room, defined by concrete surfaces and wooden furniture, reveals a hint of masculinity to balance out the emotional experience of the bright and warm kitchen traditionally considered more feminine.

↗
Maggie's Newcastle, 2013. The L-shaped building establishes a strong relationship with the surrounding nature

© Cullinan Studio

architect
Ted Cullinan
of Cullinan Studio

landscape architect
Sarah Price

construction
2012 - 2013

1. Entrance / Welcome area
2. Office
3. Large sitting room / Library
4. Kitchen
5. Courtyard
6. Group activity room
7. Consultation rooms

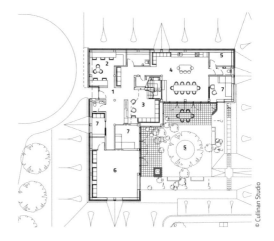

0 2 5   10 m

© Cullinan Studio

© Paul Raftery

←
The inner courtyard is home to a variety of trees and aromatic herbs

→
The staircase leading to the upper floor and terrace also serves as a bookcase

↓
Combining beauty, structure, and function, the bathed-with-sunlight central space invites us to sit on the orange bench that acts as a base of the window frame

11. Maggie's Yorkshire

St James's
University Hospital
Alma Street, Leeds LS9 7BE,
United Kingdom

Mon - Fri / 9 am - 5 pm

+44 113 4578364
leeds@maggies.org
www.maggies.org

In front of the Oncology Unit, Maggie's Yorkshire sits on a residual green corner of the hospital grounds and, responding to the context with opposite entrances on different levels, adapts to the downhill terrain. Taking advantage of the slope, visitors enjoy views of the Yorkshire Dales. Conceived as a group of three large-scale "planters" immersed in greenery, the rooftop garden features autochthonous plants alongside evergreen areas to offer visitors contact with nature all the year around. In inviting them to take care of plants, the outdoor rooms create a therapeutic environment.

After pausing on a bench carved out of a tree trunk, we enter the lower level. We find ourselves in a large space punctuated by a dense ribbed timber structure that curves seamlessly with the ceiling and envelops us. The warm tones of the wood, the porous plaster and the diffused light feed our sensorial experience. In the large fluid space, which moves between the three volumes of "planters" where several flights of comfortable stairs invite us to the different levels: if we go down one level, to the social group activity room, if instead we go up a level, we reach the kitchen; if we finally continue we will arrive at more private spaces of contemplation.

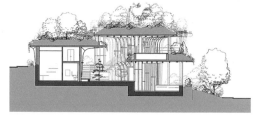

↗
Maggie's Yorkshire, 2019.
Due to the different height
of the site, the building has
two opposite entrances on
different levels

© Hufton+Crow

architect
Thomas Heatherwick
of Heatherwick Studio

landscape architect
Marie-Louise Agius
of Balston Agius

construction
2018 - 2019

1. Entrance
2. Welcome area
3. Computer desk
4. Library
5. Kitchen
6. Consultation room
7. Large sitting room /
   Group activity room

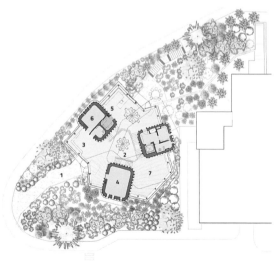

0 2   5   10 m

↖
Entering from the lower
level, we are faced with a
large space characterised by
a wooden structure running
between walls and ceiling

↑ →
The large space is connected
by a staircase that leads to
the room for group activities
(above) or to the kitchen
with the classic large table
(bottom)

12. Maggie's Oldham

The Sir Norman Stoller Building
The Royal Oldham Hospital,
Rochdale Road,
Oldham OL1 2JH,
United Kingdom

Mon - Fri / 9 am - 5 pm

+44 161 989 0550
oldham@maggies.org
www.maggies.org

Located on the northwest edge of the Royal Oldham Hospital, opposite the Breast Cancer Unit, Maggie's Oldham rises from a site that housed a former mortuary. Not used for many years, the steeply sloping site was a derelict place. Despite this, it was chosen because it was in a quieter part of the hospital with an open view of the Pennine Hills. Conceived as a raised "box" with a large hole through it, the wood and glass building stands on tall thin legs, allowing the space below to become a garden for the entire hospital. If we cross the pedestrian bridge from the parking lot of the cancer building, we find the entrance. Already visible from the bridge, a bright interior space attracts us in. As soon as we enter, a curved glass case embraces us while the silver birch tree contained within welcomes us. At the heart of the building, through the glass case, we can see the garden below and the sky above. The curved glass encourages body movement. Pushing us to the left, where another curve embraces the circular kitchen table, it leads us towards the last curve which includes a small corner where we can sit. From here we can observe the open space that offers a full sensory experience: the bright yellow floor transfers joy and energy; wood throughout, including door handles, transmits warmth.

All on one level, the building organises the rooms with function on the entrance side and an open kitchen and shelving on the opposite side. Towards the hospital, the view is mediated by

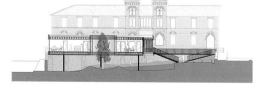

↗

Maggie's Oldham, 2017.
The building, a wooden "box" raised off the ground, houses a large garden underneath

©Jasmin Sohi

architects
Alex de Rijke and Jasmin Sohi
of dRMM Architects

landscape architect
Rupert Muldoon

construction
2016 - 2017

→
At the entrance, a large
curved glass leads us into
the interior

↘
The open sitting room,
with the infinite view to the
horizon, turns into the group
activity room where we
can also find the darkness
to sleep

the deep terrace deck facing south that, together with the niches and comfortable armchairs,
reinforces the domestic atmosphere of the
kitchen. Towards the hills, the infinite view to
the horizon transfers self-control, being able
to look far away from a safe place. If we pull
the silver curtain by Dutch artist Petra Blaisse,
the large sitting room with freestanding fireplace turns into the group activity room; a private circular space where it is dark enough for
a nap during group relaxation or alone.
In the cantilevered structure, the world's first
hardwood CLT (cross-laminated timber) building,
the construction rationale is precise. Tulipwood
walls, plywood, cork and other natural materials including wood fibre insulation make this a
healthy building. Its therapeutic nature continues in the garden and greenhouse. Connected
to the terrace by a staircase, the garden invites
us to enjoy its calm atmosphere, and when it
rains heavily to watch water fall into a reflec-
tive bowl that collects rain from the roof. The
greenhouse encourages visitors to look after
the flowers and vegetables and to share their
food and emotions.

1. Entrance
2. Welcome area
3. Kitchen
4. Library / Computer desk
5. Consultation rooms
6. Office
7. Large sitting room /
   Group acitivity room
8. Silver birch tree

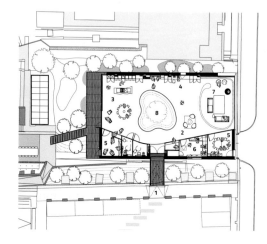

0 2   5 m ⊕

13. Maggie's Manchester

The Robert Parfett Building
The Christie Hospital N H S
Foundation Trust,
15 Kinnaird Road,
Manchester M20 4QL,
United Kingdom

Mon - Fri / 9 am - 5 pm

+44 161 641 4848
manchester@maggies.org
www.maggies.org

At the end of the avenue opposite the hospital, on the site of a former car park, Maggie's Manchester is a pavilion in the garden. This new oasis follows Foster + Partners' idea to incorporate nature into the building as part of the healing process. To make the most of the sun exposure, the garden occupies the southern part of the site, while the building occupies the northern part so as to be more connected with the road. Derived from the rectangular shape of the site, the linear building has a wide veranda at the front, reminiscent of an American porch, where people can enjoy the outdoor space even when it rains. We can pause in this transitional spot before entering.

Inside, a bright and airy space punctuated by a light timber structure reminds us of an aircraft hangar. Here, the architecture is so transparent that we have to refer to the scale of the furniture: the bench by the entrance, the kitchen counter, the kitchen table, the sitting room. As we walk, we realise that our level of safety increases and the orderly structure of space helps us organise our minds and offers a sense of calm. The net curtains also help minimise the glare, giving a sense of privacy, which can change when they open, creating a domestic environment.

Almost twice as big as earlier centres, Maggie's Manchester has all the "ingredients" that constitute the DNA of a Maggie's centre: open layout, extra height, daylight, besides the use of natural materials, very discreet lights, and the

↗
Maggie's Manchester, 2016.
The linear building makes the most of the sun exposure by incorporating nature into it, starting from its diamond-shaped greenhouse

© Foster + Partners

architects
Foster + Partners

landscape architect
Dan Pearson

construction
2015 - 2016

→
As soon as we enter, a bright and airy space with a rhythmic light wooden structure reminds us of an aerial hangar

↘
The greenhouse, used all year round, is a space where visitors can take care of the plants

transparency that, in this case, allows the staff to look down from the mezzanine level. Upstairs, as well as the office space, little secret spaces such as the wig corner allow us to hide. The central spine containing the stairs, toilets and store rooms organises the building into public, open spaces to the west and private consultation rooms, which overlook outdoor courtyards, to the east.

With biophilic references, wood has been used effectively and efficiently to give the building its character, expressing it through the shape of the structure. After all unnecessary material having been removed, LVL (laminated veneer lumber) is like a kit whose sheets are cut and glued together in four components. The apotheosis of the structural system is symbolically represented by the diamond-shaped greenhouse. Here visitors can enjoy the therapeutic qualities of nature while taking care of plants and choosing flowers to bring inside, a good way to entertain people while helping them communicate. The greenhouse is used all year round and in the summer months the table on wheels can be taken out creating an additional opportunity to socialise.

1. Entrance
2. Welcome area / Library
3. Kitchen
4. Sitting rooms / Fireplace
5. Office
6. Large sitting room
7. Consultation rooms
8. Greenhouse
9. Garden

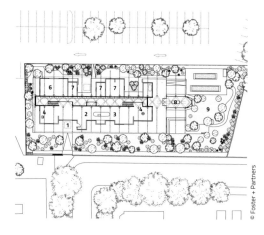

© Foster + Partners

0   5   20 m ⊘

Itinerary C
The Midlands /
Central England

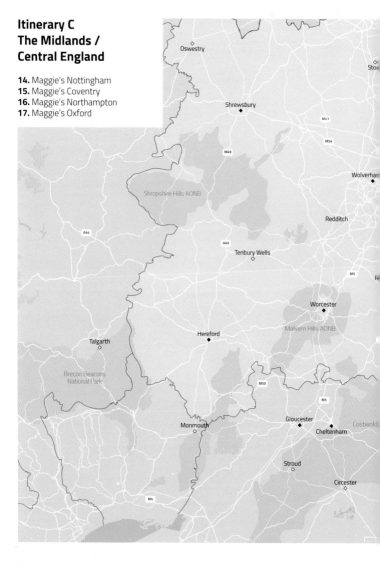

Oswestry

Sto

Shrewsbury

M41

M54

Wolverha

Shropshire Hills AONB

Redditch

A44

A49

Tenbury Wells

M5

Worcester

Malvern Hills AONB

Talgarth

Hereford

Brecon Beacons
National Park

M50

M5

Monmouth

Gloucester

Cheltenham

Costwold

Stroud

Circester

M4

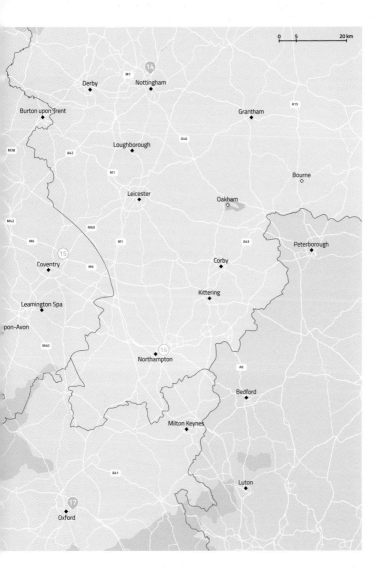

0   5   20 km

M1

Derby

Nottingham

Burton upon Trent

M38

A42

Loughborough

M1

Leicester

M42

M6

M69

M1

15

Coventry

M6

Leamington Spa

pon-Avon

M40

16

Northampton

A41

17

Oxford

14

Grantham

A15

A46

Bourne

Oakham

A43

Peterborough

Corby

Kittering

A6

Bedford

Milton Keynes

Luton

14. Maggie's Nottingham

City Hospital Campus
Nottingham City Hospital
Hucknall Road,
Nottingham NG5 1PH,
United Kingdom

Mon - Fri / 9 am - 5 pm

+44 115 924 6210
nottingham@maggies.org
www.maggies.org

On a steep site near the Oncology Unit, chosen because the hospital would have had no interest in using it, Maggie's Nottingham is a highly visible object despite being immersed in nature. A simple concept, a square box inspired by Canadian log cabins characterised by their interlocking corners was transformed when the façades were made oval and the interlocking parts became large "ears". Amusing and light-hearted, the green egg that is Maggie's Nottingham welcomes visitors at the door and makes them smile.

To make it easily accessible on foot from the oncological unit, the entrance is at the top of the hill. Entering at an elevated level, visitors will be so high up that they can "shake hands with the trees". Almost a tree house, Maggie's Nottingham is simultaneously "refuge" and "prospect", making people feel safe, while giving them a 360-degree view. Indeed, the separate balconies on each side – of which the south terrace becomes an outdoor room – recall, as Charles Jencks had guessed, the Palladian Rotund, which with its square layout offers the same opening with different views of the landscape. The price for having a little tree house is that the garden is more distant, but on sunny days, this invites users to come out and enjoy the enchanting view from the long entrance bench, where visitors can pause before entering.

The door allows for a discreet entrance. Like for Maggie's visitors, when we enter, we will be seen and welcomed by the Staff. Then, we will either

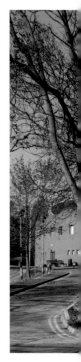

Maggie's Nottingham, 2011.
The curious green box positioned on a sloping terrain welcomes visitors by emerging from the vegetation

© CZWG Limited

© Martine Hamilton Knight

architects
Piers Gough of CZWG
Architects; Paul Smith Ltd
(interior design)

landscape architect
Geoff Southern of CZWG
Architects

construction
2010 - 2011

→
The kitchen room is a gathering place from which one can reach the adjacent rooms and find privacy

↘
Connected to the kitchen, the south terrace becomes an open room where visitors will be so high up that they can "shake hands with the trees"

enter the library on the right or go down to the kitchen. In line with the geometry of the building, the kitchen is located in the centre at the bottom of the oval and, going down, the feeling is that of passing through a narrow alley and arriving in a square where people meet. Designed not for sitting alone but to facilitate contact and conversation, the smaller-than-usual kitchen is, however, connected to side rooms where people can find some privacy while still feeling included through interior openings.

Without indulging in double-height spaces and aiming to be an unexpensive building, Maggie's Nottingham is a traditional house with separate rooms and open doors, although the compact space opens up in the staircase featuring landings in the manner of Adolf Loos's half-levels. Upstairs, the consultation rooms, of different colours and arranged symmetrically with respect to the staircase, precede the group activity room divisible into two. Even if the audacity of the exterior makes no hint of it, inside the visitor will find a domestic space that offers the pleasure of "feeling at home" in a lovely house. With interiors designed by Paul Smith, known for being drawn to old-fashioned comfort, the building has "a traditional look with a twist", evident in the chairs upholstered in his colourful and refined design fabric.

1. Entrance
2. Welcome area / Library
3. Office
4. Kitchen
5. Sitting rooms
6. Terrace

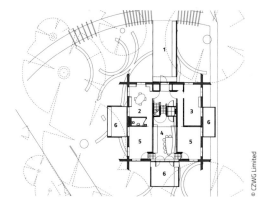

0 2 5 10 m

© CZWG Limited

15. Maggie's Coventry

University Hospitals Coventry & Warwickshire
Clifford Bridge Road,
Coventry CV2 2DX,
United Kingdom

annette.cameron@maggies.org
www.maggies.org

Maggie's Coventry is situated on a gentle hill at the very edge of the University Hospitals Coventry & Warwickshire grounds. As we approach it, crossing a public garden, we have a view to the north, across a wide expanse of green countryside stretching out to the beautiful pine forests beyond. Leaving behind the massive infrastructure and hard landscaping of the hospital complex, this wonderful location in the landscape makes us feel we have arrived in a place which feels entirely set apart, an oasis of peace. Set low in the site, the building is loosely arranged among a series of 'secret' sunken gardens. As we approach, its three glazed volumes beckon us and invite us in.

On entering the heart of the building, the three light-filled volumes, equal in scale but varied in proportions, welcome us under a canopy of natural light that unites the centre's communal areas. Open and free of internal walls, this core space allows us to move easily from the kitchen to the large sitting room and to the library, creating a very domestic atmosphere. While the tea is brewing, we can sit and chat with people making ourself at home or enter the surrounding, more secluded rooms to relax, read a book or just take a nap. From each room we will be able to enjoy the view of a different garden, always making us feel comfortable, welcomed and uplifted.

→
Maggie's Coventry, ongoing. Firmly embedded in the beautiful landscape, with a reassuring perspective on the peace of the countryside, the building is a place that makes visitors feel set apart and in control

© Jamie Fobert Architects

architects
Jamie Fobert
of Jamie Fobert Architects

landscape architect
Nigel Dunnett

construction
in development

16. Maggie's Northampton

Northampton General Hospital NHS Trust
Cliftonville,
Northampton NN1 5BD,
United Kingdom

annette.cameron@maggies.org
www.maggies.org

Maggie's Northampton is easy to find within the huge regional hospital complex; we can recognise it from a distance thanks to its pyramid roof. Finished with white perforated panels that extend beyond the edge of the building, like a floating umbrella, the roof overlaps the fully glazed perimeter to provide shade. The garden surrounding the building includes topiary at right angles that when viewed from inside will look like extensions of the interior spaces; the walls of the entire perimeter of the new building are made of glass to allow us views in a seamless link between inside and outside. In contrast with the glass, an oak door clearly indicates the entrance.

Once inside, we are greeted by the bright double-height central space of the library, from where we can move easily to the surrounding areas depending on whether we are more attracted to the cheerful noise coming from the kitchen or the calmer atmosphere of the large living room. As we continue, we realise that the concrete floor finish extends outdoors to form a tray for sitting – very much like a beach. This tray extends to contain a larger seating area with pools, and also folds up to form a wall with cascades which will be lit at night to form the background to the inner life of the centre. Even if we arrive on a late November afternoon, the garden will always invite us to linger in this open-air sensory room.

→
Maggie's Northampton, ongoing.
Despite the complex setting of a busy regional hospital, the building is easy to recognise for its unconventional roof that inspires protection and tranquility

90

© Stephen Marshall Architects

architects
Stephen Marshall Architects

landscape architect
Arne Maynard

construction
in development

17. Maggie's Oxford

The Patricia Thompson Building, Churchill Hospital
Old Road, Oxford OX3 7LE, United Kingdom

Mon - Fri / 9 am - 5 pm

+44 1865 751882
oxford@maggies.org
www.maggies.org

Opposite the Oncology Unit, Maggie's Oxford is located on the border between the hospital and a nature reserve. Designed as a tree house immersed in the surrounding foliage, the building is set back from the road and, rising lightly from a drop in the ground, emerges as a one-storey volume, in perfect harmony with the context. Speaking the refined language of nature, the building, based on a leaf-shaped three-pronged plan and delimited by a series of planes, roots its structure among the existing trees and significantly increases the length of the façade that alternates solid concrete walls with glass and with protective wooden grids.

Crossing the bridge, where we still have the time to reflect, we reach the entrance. Welcomed by cheerful yellow details in walls and furniture, we realise that at the heart of the building, the triangular kitchen table follows the shape of the space which, by including the adjacent fireplace area, reinforces the domestic atmosphere and allows people to feel involved, yet being secluded. Although it has rooms but with an open-plan feel, the interior space plays on transparency and the wooden finishes attract the eye and exude a sense of warmth. Open to nature, the sitting room at the end of this wing culminates in a terrace that connects to the other terraces and the garden beneath the building.

↗

Maggie's Oxford, 2014. The building, detached from the road, invites us to cross the bridge and reach the front door

architects
Chris Wilkinson
of WilkinsonEyre

landscape architect
Flora Gathorne-Hardy

construction
2013 - 2014

1. Entrance
2. Welcome area / Library
3. Office
4. Kitchen
5. Consultation rooms
6. Large sitting room /
   Group activity room
7. Garden

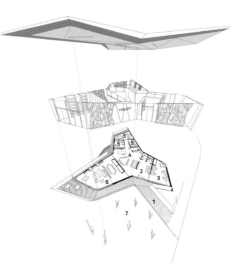

← →
As soon as we enter, the bright space will welcome us in the centre of the building characterised by the big triangular kitchen table and the adjacent fireplace area that reinforce the domestic atmosphere

↓
The wooden finishes of the living room in strong relationship with nature reinforce a sense of warmth and therapeutic effects

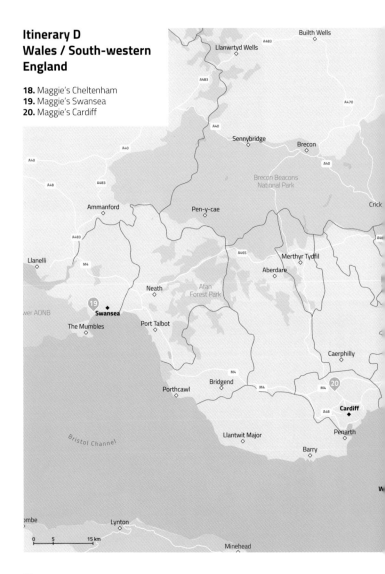

Itinerary D
Wales / South-western England

Builth Wells

Llanwrtyd Wells

A483

A483

A483

A470

A40

A40

A40

Sennybridge

Brecon

A40

A48

A483

Brecon Beacons
National Park

Ammanford

Pen-y-cae

Crick

A483

A465

Merthyr Tydfil

Llanelli

M4

Aberdare

Neath

Afan
Forest Park

wer AONB

Swansea

19

The Mumbles

Port Talbot

Caerphilly

M4

Bridgend

Porthcawl

M4

M4

20

Cardiff

A48

Penarth

Bristol Channel

Llantwit Major

Barry

W

ombe

Lynton

0   5   15 km

Minehead

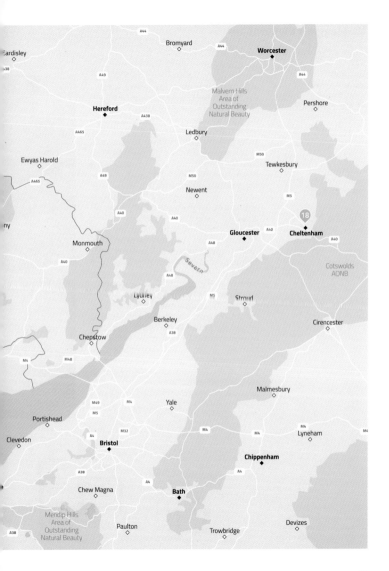

18. Maggie's Cheltenham

**Cheltenham
General Hospital**
College Baths Road,
Cheltenham GL53 7QB,
United Kingdom

Mon - Fri / 9 am - 5 pm

+44 1242 250611
cheltenham@maggies.org
www.maggies.org

Incorporating a Victorian lodge formerly part of the hospital, Maggie's Cheltenham is located along the River Chelt, once known for its beneficial springs. Out of all the Maggie's centres, this is the only one where an old building coexists with a new one, complementing each other and creating a variety of intimate outdoor spaces that improve the site and acknowledge the presence of the river through the addition of a terrace. A long sculptural fountain made of stainless-steel pipes accompanies us to the entrance pergola, which takes us into a "secret" garden: surprised by the green and flowery space we pose for a moment before entering.

Located between the two buildings, the bright entrance takes us straight to the heart of the centre. Wrightian-inspired, MJP Architects' building incorporates the concept of "prospect" and "refuge", solid yet open to the outside, while the roof appears to float above a thin, horizontal strip of natural light. Conceived as a single room, the space subsequently transforms from kitchen area to inglenook lit from above, to group activity room. Along the habitable walls, two openings overlook welcoming semi-circular alcoves. Inside, we find a comforting space that leaves room for discovery and imagination. Using warm colours, calibrated on the human scale, this masterpiece in carpentry ends with a refined large sitting room which creates a calm domestic atmosphere.

↗
Maggie's Cheltenham, 2010.
The new building and the old
one coexist, creating a series
of outdoor spaces where you
can relax and enjoy nature

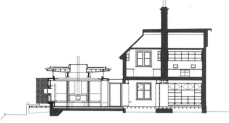

© Peter Durant

architect
Sir Richard MacCormac
of MJP Architects

landscape architect
Dr Christine Facer

construction
2009 - 2010

1. Entrance
2. Welcome area / Library
3. Large sitting room with fireplace / Group activity room
4. Kitchen
5. Consultation rooms
6. Inglenook lit from above
7. "Secret" garden

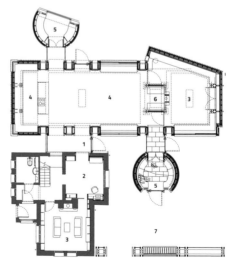

0   2   5 m

←
Maggie's Cheltenham is located near the River Chelt, which we can admire from the new terrace

→
Located between the two buildings, the bright entrance takes us from the new building to the old one

↓
The space of the kitchen, designed as a large room, becomes an inglenook lit from above and, beyond, a group activity area

19. Maggie's Swansea

Singleton Hospital
Sketty Lane, Sketty,
Swansea SA2 8QL,
United Kingdom

Mon - Fri / 9 am - 5 pm

+44 1792 200000
swansea@maggies.org
www.maggies.org

For Kishō Kurokawa, who suddenly passed away in 2007, life was a small universe, a cosmos in constant movement that generates swirling energy. At Maggie's Swansea, his original concept of spiral movement was faithfully developed by Garbers & James who, in finalising the geometry of the elliptical drum, paid particular attention to the two tapered and curved wings, which are not a simple extrusion of the main body but maintain their own nature, precisely because we know that "energy is in the tail". The idea of the universe of stars is also highlighted by the insertion of titanium chips in the concrete façade. Previously used by Kurokawa in his Roman Art Museum in Japan, the chips representing the shells that move under the light work well in Swansea too, where the weather conditions change constantly reflecting a wide range of colours ranging from dark green sea to the royal blue sky. The fact that Swansea is immersed in nature also means that Maggie's Swansea offers, as the Brief requires, external views with different points of view and perspectives on the horizon. So, from the large mezzanine window we can see the sea in the distance, from the small windows to the north we are projected towards the beautiful trees of the neighbouring park, and if we walk outside we find ourselves immersed in the sophisticated landscape of vegetable gardens, with interspersed patterns of textures, colours and scents.

↗
Maggie's Swansea, 2011.
Immersed in nature, the building is a small universe of stars, many flakes of bright titanium fused in the concrete façade that embraces us with its wing and invites us to enter

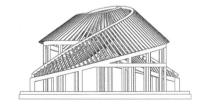

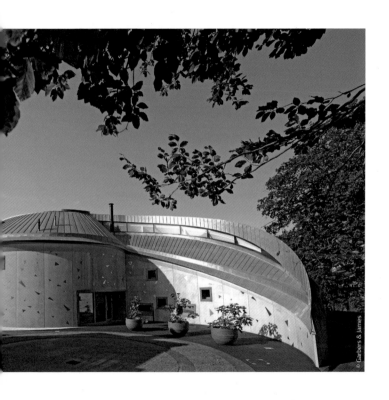

© Garbers & James

architects
Kishō Kurokawa Architects
with Garbers & James

landscape architect
Kim Wilkie

construction
2010 - 2011

→
From the large window of the mezzanine, our infinite view of the horizon reaches the sea in the distance

↘
Downstairs, the large space dominated by the oculus above intersects with the intimate kitchen area

The holistic nature of Maggie's Swansea can be felt from the moment we are "embraced" by its right wing and invited to enter. Inside, the large space is dominated by the oculus above, at the centre of the spiral from which all energy radiates. Following Murphy's design principle, established at Maggie's Edinburgh, this open space intersects the intimate kitchen area where visitors gather around the table, sharing their lives over a cup of tea. The leaf-shaped table allows for different types of conversations: confidential, one-to-one at its tip, or a group discussion on the opposite side by the large rounded end. Reinforcing the atmosphere of openness fundamental to Maggie's philosophy, the open kitchen shelves invite people to help themselves and feel at home. Inside the large entrance space, a curved flight of stairs takes us to the mezzanine floor which can also be accessed by lift. The consultation and group activity rooms, the library and the office are therefore accessible to everyone, also ensuring order and organisation, the latter made easier by lots of storage space.

1. Entrance
2. Welcome area
3. Fireplace
4. Kitchen
5. Computer desk
6. Consultation rooms
7. Large sitting room
8. Terrace

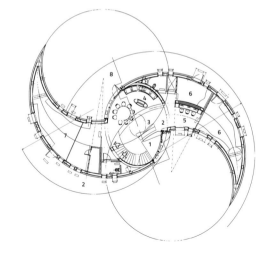

0   2   5 m

20. Maggie's Cardiff

The Chris McGuigan Building
Velindre Cancer Centre
Velindre Road, Whitchurch
Cardiff CF14 2TL,
United Kingdom

Mon - Fri / 9 am - 5 pm

+44 29 2240 8024
cardiff@maggies.org
www.maggies.org

Maggie's Cardiff is located at the bottom of the Velindre Cancer Centre car park. Despite the uninspiring context and the apparently modest character of a tin shed, the building impresses with its monochromatic compositional elegance of its shaped profile that recalls both the neighboring houses and the hills on the horizon. Occupying the entire site, the building extends with a tail towards the west, improving the geometry of its plan and establishing a close relationship with the nature at the back. On the urban side, as if protecting the building against cars, the site boundary is delimited by a row of cast iron bollards designed by the artist Antony Gormley. The open corner invites us to a quiet entrance courtyard where we can "pause" and think for a moment.

Inside, the wood finishes contribute to the familiar atmosphere. The kitchen, at the centre of the building, is a dynamic space, with its pitched white metal ceiling rising and directing our eyes toward the outdoor terrace and landscape. Opposite, a series of consultation rooms reaches intimacy through coloured curtains. In the centre, the *cwtch*, inspired by the chimneys of Welsh vernacular architecture, welcomes us to an intimate space illuminated by a skylight. The building is enriched by many works of art by various artists. The *Self Portrait* by Osi Rhys Osmond generates a mnemonic relationship between art and the daily life of Maggie's users.

↗
Maggie's Cardiff, 2019.
The building is a
monochromatic volume
with pitched roofs, bordered
by Antony Gormley's corten
bollards that protect it from
the street

© Dow Jones

architects
Biba Dow and Alun Jones
of Dow Jones Architects

landscape architect
Cleve West

construction
2018 - 2019

1. Entrance courtyard
2. Office
3. Consultation rooms
4. Large sitting room /
   Group activity room
5. Kitchen
6. *Cwtch*
7. Library
8. Terrace

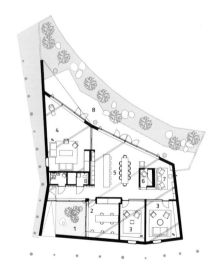

0 2 5 m

■
The exposed roof pitches give character to the different spaces of the building, particularly in the kitchen where our gaze is drawn from the woods

↑
Seamlessly, from the kitchen we pass into the large living room that overlooks the external terrace

→
Emphasising the irregular geometry of the building, the roof pitches rotated by 45 degrees with respect to the plan enliven the space, improving its brightness, especially evident in the large sitting room

Itinerary E
Greater London /
Eastern England /
Southern England

21. Maggie's Southampton
22. Maggie's at The Royal Marsden
23. Maggie's West London
24. Maggie's Barts – London
    (City & East)
25. Maggie's at The Royal Free

Worcester
Leamington Spa
Stratford-upon-Avon
North
M45
M40
A43
A46
M5
A44
Cheltenham
A34
A41
Costswolds
AONB
Oxford
Cirencester
M40
Malmesbury
Chiltern Hills
AONB
M4
M4
Swindon
Bristol
Chippenham
M4
North Wessex Downs
AONB
Bath
A39
A34
Reading
A36
M4
A33
M3
A36
A31
Salisbury
A34
Cranborne Chase
AONB
Winchester
A36
21
A3
South Downs
National Park
M27
A31
Southampton
A31
A35
Burnemouth
Portsmouth
Isle of Wight
Shanklin
Ventnor
English Channel

21. Maggie's Southampton

Southampton General Hospital
Tremona Road,
Southampton SO16 6YD,
United Kingdom

+44 238 212 4549
southampton@
maggiescentres.org
www.maggies.org

In the hospital grounds, Maggie's Southampton occupies a corner of a former parking lot. With the idea of transporting a haven of a garden from the New Forest to the concrete landscape of the hospital, the building emerges from the earth camouflaging its roof with the surrounding nature. The arboreal context and the wild naturalistic topography that derive from it offer us an oasis of peace and safety that protects us from the outside world. Avoiding following the grid of the large hospital blocks, the building, based on a four-walled pinwheel system, rotates and, lengthening a wall, invites us to pause before entering.

The large earth-coloured ceramic wall takes us directly to the heart of the centre. Here, the kitchen table lit from above welcomes us, making us feel immediately at home. Thanks to the rotation, the central space offers glimpses of nature and open views on the most private spaces contained in the four wings of the building. Even if we retreat to more private areas, the opening of the space, divided only by sliding walls and a mobile threshold between the interior and the garden, makes us feel part of the whole. Back outside, the consulting rooms, covered in mirrored glass, seem to disappear while reflecting the trees and planting.

↗
Maggie's Southampton, 2021.
As if transported from the New Forest to the hospital's concrete landscape, the camouflaged haven covered with mirrored glass seems to disappear as it reflects the surrounding new trees and planting

© Hufton+Crow

architects	landscape architect	construction
AL_A	Sarah Price	2019 - 2021

1. Entrance
2. Welcome area
3. Office
4. Kitchen
5. Library / Computer desk
6. Large sitting room /
   Group activity room
7. Counsultation rooms
8. Large sitting room
9. Garden

0 2 5   10 m

↖
Occupying a corner of a former parking lot, the building is nudged off axis with the big hospital block and appears as something apart and special

↑
A central space is formed by a gap as the four structural walls approach, with private spaces spinning from the open kitchen area

→
Social and semi-social spaces are porous, divided only by sliding partitions and a moveable threshold between interior and exterior

22. Maggie's at The Royal Marsden

The Royal Marsden Hospital
17 Cotswold Road,
Sutton SM2 5NG,
United Kingdom

Mon - Fri / 9 am - 5 pm

+44 20 3982 3141
maggies.royalmarsden
@maggies.org
www.maggies.org

On the edge of the hospital grounds, but not in the immediate vicinity of the Oncology Unit, Maggie's at The Royal Marsden is a little difficult to find. Following the signs and crossing the parking lot, we arrive in a new landscape from which a series of escalating volumes cladded in terracotta, in different shades of red, emerges. Conceived together, the fan-shaped building and the circular landscape complement each other by wrapping themselves around a quiet central courtyard, all surrounded by centuries-old trees. Walking towards the building, we feel the relationship between landscape and interior spaces through the large windows that encourage us to enter.

Once inside, we are greeted by a quiet welcome area, while the colours and natural light guide us towards the double-height space of the kitchen. Here, the large table invites us to sit and drink a cup of tea with the other visitors, making us feel at home. Looking at the red stairs we experience swirling sensations. Going up the stairs, we notice that the sequence of our movement follows the movement of the sun, which enters the building animating it. From above, the view on the space joins the one on the outside and, through the great transparencies, connects us with the surrounding landscape.

↗
Maggie's at The Royal
Marsden, 2019.
The fan-shaped building
wraps around a central
courtyard surrounded by
centuries-old trees

architects
Ab Rogers Design

landscape architect
Piet Oudolf

construction
2017 - 2019

→
A palette of colours and natural light guide us through the building where each room has a different tint; here the bright yellow of the fireplace room expresses energy and warmth

→
Fully glazed walls allow for total continuity between outside and inside

↘
Below, the large kitchen table, contained by the swirling red stairs, invites us to sit and have tea with the other visitors

1. Entrance
2. Welcome area / Library
3. Kitchen
4. Sitting room / Fireplace
5. Consultation rooms
6. Living room
7. Garden house

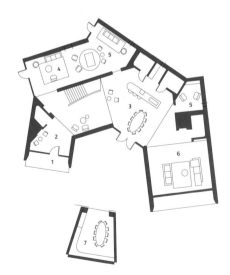

0   2   5 m

23. Maggie's West London

Charing Cross Hospital
Fulham Palace Road,
London W6 8RF,
United Kingdom

Mon - Fri / 9 am - 5 pm

+44 20 7386 1750
london@maggies.org
www.maggies.org

Located on a former municipal green in front of the hospital, Maggie's West London seems to be the natural answer to the site. Like a gatehouse that might be read as a sculpture in a garden, the bright orange building protects its visitors from the traffic noise of the city, offering an oasis of calm. In an attempt to influence its surroundings, the solid but warm wall extends from the nautilus-like design, inviting us to enter. This slow procession helps us to "pause" at a series of thresholds: through the window we see where we are going; we wait a moment to understand if this is the positive move to make; in the end we decide to proceed. Following the path between the two high walls, we stop at the end. On the left, a new window, this time blurry, reminds us of the city we leave to enter, on the right, into another world. If from the outside the building seemed closed, once inside, there is a completely different atmosphere. The grid structure allows a 360-degree perspective, conveying a sense of transparency. Despite the hard, cold materiality of the columns and concrete floor, what we feel is the openness of the building and its evolving space. The use of sliding doors, which can be left slightly open, reinforces space continuity. In this uninterrupted space, what defines the individual moments are the bookshelves, which reinforce the unity of space through their uniform material treatment, becoming a neutral background for the activities.

↗
Maggie's West London, 2008. Protected by a large floating roof and a high bright orange wall, the building seems to want to escape the outside world, but the window through which we glimpse the internal garden intrigues us and invites us to enter

© Rogers Stirk Harbour + Partners, (RSHP)

architects
Ivan Harbour of Rogers
Stirk Harbour + Partners

landscape architect
Dan Pearson

construction
2007 - 2008

→
The window puts in contact
the garden and the external
courtyard, which offers
areas of sun and shade and
a "prospect and refuge"
experience

↘
Despite the cold materiality
of the concrete, what we
feel is the spatial continuity
reinforced by the continuous
treatment of the warm wood
finishes, becoming a neutral
background for the activities

In addition to the continuity of the material, there is also a continuity of light. If we look up, we can see the ceiling, a large lantern that brings in natural light and, at the same time, reduce the visual impact of the hospital tower. Although the original idea was that the upper floor be used solely for administrative operations, it was very quickly adapted for the activities of the centre, despite having no lift access. Also, if we look around, we will not find any sign, not even escape signs. As a fundamental part of the Maggie's Architectural Brief, this strengthens the perception of the garden pavilion appearing as a non-institutional building in a bustling, institutional environment.

The outdoor spaces are the result of the garden wall that united to the building wraps around itself forming the open courtyard. Inspired by Maggie's study of the Chinese Garden, this garden offers areas of sun and shadow, where we find intimate spaces and peace. Here, the warm orange wall and the contact with the outside world reappear. Mentally retracing the route that we took this far in search of a restorative space, we now feel we are in a safe place from which we can look out appreciating the meandering path in the landscape designed by Dan Pearson that led us here.

1. Entrance
2. Welcome area / Library
3. Kitchen / Fireplace
4. Large sitting room /
   Group activity room
5. Consultation rooms
6. Courtyard
7. Path

0   5   20 m ↻

© 2022 Ben Blossom

© Morley von Sternberg, courtesy of Rogers Stirk Harbour + Partners

24. Maggie's Barts – London (City & East)

St Bartholomew's Hospital
W Smithfield,
London EC1A 7BE,
United Kingdom

Mon - Fri / 9 am - 5 pm

+44 20 3904 3448
barts@maggies.org
www.maggies.org

Standing at the corner of the courtyard of the historic St Bartholomew's Hospital in London, Maggie's Barts is connected to James Gibbs' 18th-century North Wing, known for the Hogarth Stair and the Great Hall. Inspired by the colourful notes of the '*neume* notation' of medieval music of the 13th century, the façade introduces coloured fragments as notes in a pentagram. To give the score continuity, the façade features rounded corners on all sides including where the new building meets the old building, so as to reveal its rustic quoins. The façade, by day opaque, at night lights up and, like a lantern, transmits positive energy. The centre has two entrances, one facing the chapel of St Bartholomew-the-Less and the other, the main entrance, in the historic courtyard. This is where we enter.

Having paused at the entrance, once inside we realise that Maggie's Barts is breathtaking. In the double-height space, the white translucent glass façade punctuated by various bright colours diffuses a calm, warm light. In addition to the external layer, we discover the layer of the structure conceived as a concrete frame that tilts along with the musical notation. A third layer is that of the bamboo stairs, which acts like a warm embrace.

Light, space, and shape are all elements that enrich our sensory experience but, going beyond the five senses, they convey sensations of orientation, balance and movement. This is what

↗
Maggie's Barts – London (City and East), 2017. Thanks to its stunning glass façade, the 'urban' Maggie's offers a totally different visual experience from the rest of the context, especially at night when it becomes a luminous lantern for the entire hospital courtyard

© Iwan Baan

architects
Steven Holl Architects and
Darren Hawkes (future
extension)

landscape architect
Darren Hawkes

construction
2015 - 2017

125

The opalescent glass shields
us from outside view except
for a single transparent
window

↘

Thanks to the warmth of the
wood the building feels like a
large house

we feel as we climb the stairs of Maggie's Barts.
The building, quite contained in plan, develops vertically on three floors so as to feel like
a large house. Thanks to the way we come in,
prepare our cup of tea and sit at the table, we
find a great sense of domesticity within the
kitchen area. When we look at it from above,
the table, at the centre, becomes a reference
point for the entire building. Designed with an
hourglass shape, depending on where and how
we sit, it can accommodate multiple conversations of various kinds.

In seeking visual separation from the hospital,
the translucent glass prevents us from seeing
outside. While walking up the stairs, however,
we discover a transparent window overlooking the square and when we finally get to the
top, all the windows overlooking the terrace are
transparent, putting us in contact with nature.
The large tree behind the apse of the church
reveals the change of seasons and, interacting
with the architecture, it reinforces the therapeutic role of the building. The view over the
roofs of the surrounding buildings makes us
feel protected, far from the city, almost in an
English village. But if we look far beyond the
hospital, the view on the horizon makes us feel
optimistic about the future.

1. Entrance
2. Welcome area
3. Sitting areas
4. Kitchen
5. Consultation room

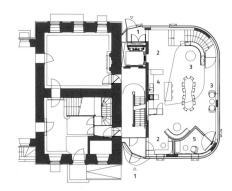

0   2   5 m

25. Maggie's at The Royal Free

The Royal Free Hospital
Pond Street,
London NW3 2QG,
United Kingdom

Mon - Fri / 9 am - 5 pm

royalfree@maggies.org
www.maggies.org

Located on the southwest corner of The Royal Free Hospital car park, Maggie's at The Royal Free constitutes a strong presence even from afar. In contrast with the clinical built environment, aseptic and boxy, its undulating timber form beckons and draws us inside as we approach the building. The structure has a small footprint on ground level but expands in form as the building rises. This fact tells us that the potential of the site has been maximised by creating extra space in the garden, offering people with cancer a quiet zone to pause before entering.

Just after crossing the threshold, we are greeted by a quiet welcome area where the natural light is diffused by the roof garden skylights and filtered by the timber louvres forming the façade. Designed as shading devices, the vertical elements are oriented to create intimate spaces, providing a sense of protection, but also to frame glimpses towards the outside. The internal spaces flow freely from one area to another, alternating moments of repose with dynamic movement to give us a sense of empowerment and worth. Both the form and the materials express a nurturing quality of the building that reaches its greatest impact in the peaceful outdoor retreat on the rooftop.

↗
Maggie's at The Royal Free, ongoing.
Thanks to the flared shape of the building, the garden on the ground floor expands with both soft and hardscape areas. An additional garden is located at roof level to create a serene enclosure and outdoor retreat that aligns with the canopies of the surrounding foliage

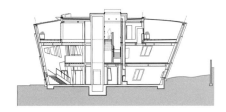

©Studio Libeskind

architect
Daniel Libeskind
of Studio Libeskind

landscape architect
Martha Schwartz

construction
in development

1. Entrance
2. Welcome area
3. Kitchen
4. Sitting area
5. Library / Large sitting room
6. Exterior sitting area

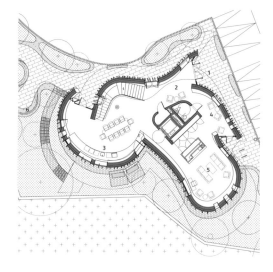

0 2   5 m

┌
The undulating timber building is nestled into a planted garden offering an oasis of peace and quiet seating

↑
Interior spaces flow freely from one to the next moved by the natural light ushered in from the roof garden skylights above

→
Intimate spaces within the interior are located along the building perimeter enabling moments of quiet and repose

Itinerary F
Europe / Asia

26. Kálida Barcelona

Kálida Barcelona
Hospital Sant Pau,
89 Carrer Sant Quintí,
Barcelona 08026, Spain

Mon - Thu / 8.30 am - 5 pm
Fri / 8.30 am - 3 pm

+34 935 537 930
hola@fundaciokalida.org
www.fundaciokalida.org

Opposite the modern Oncology Unit between the old Hospital de la Santa Creu i Sant Pau (1901-1930), modernist masterpiece by Lluís Domènech i Montaner, and the new hospital block, Kálida Barcelona has a long history that began as an idea without a site. Being the first Maggie's centre in Europe, it took a group of determined women a long time to get the project off the ground. The "non-site" at the back of the hospital that was finally offered for the project was turned into a paradise. To enter, we will first have to go through the garden, maybe take a pause, and then discover the hidden entrance. When we enter, we will feel we have chanced upon a secret haven.

Once inside, we will be struck by the strong light that filters through the large windows that connect the interior to the garden, sensing that we are in a welcoming, reassuring place. If we start wandering, we discover that each room has its own outdoor space that the atmosphere created by sunlight, dry stone walls and vegetation turns into real outdoor rooms. In the kitchen, we will be invited to prepare our cup of tea ourselves. If we don't want to sit at the large table, there is room for seclusion in the more intimate and protected corners.

Staff upstairs will have heard us enter and, just by using their voice, they will invite us to walk up the stairs or take the lift. The double-height space at the centre allows people to converse between the two floors, as they

↗
Kálida Barcelona, 2019.
Inspired by the nearby Hospital de la Santa Creu i Sant Pau, a modernist masterpiece by Lluís Domènec i Montaner, the brick building extends its spaces outside under the red leaf-shaped pergolas and in the green of the new vegetation

© Duccio Malagamba

architects
Benedetta Tagliabue
and Joan Callís
of Miralles Tagliabue EMBT

landscape architects
Miralles Tagliabue EMBT

construction
2018 - 2019

→

The large living room on the
upper floor can accommodate
various group activities

↘

Downstairs, we can sit at
the kitchen table, in the
centre of the double-height
space, or seclude ourselves
in more sheltered spaces.
As in a house, from here
we can communicate with
the people above

would in a domestic setting, making them feel
connected and included. Upstairs, in the large
sitting room, sliding doors divide the flexible
space to host multiple activities, while the Catalan vaults, following the roof line, enliven the
typical ceiling of this region.

Inspired by natural motifs and colours found in
the ceramics used in Catalan modernist architecture, the brick building has a leaf-shaped
plan. Generating a sense of protection, and at
the same time a deep perspective, the living
space extends to the splendid pergolas, bench-
es, trees and vegetation outside. In the garden, visitors can enjoy the therapeutic effect
of the wonderful climate of Barcelona, while
being immersed in the garden reminds us of
the decoration of the old hospital, replete with
leaves and flowers. Looking at the brick façade
we see that it has holes and flower and cloud
motifs thanks to a simple white patina that
allows for a sublime effect that almost whis-
pers. And if we stop and listen, we might hear
it talking to us.

1. Entrance
2. Welcome area /
   Library
3. Kitchen
4. Sitting room
5. Group activity room
6. Courtyard
7. Garden

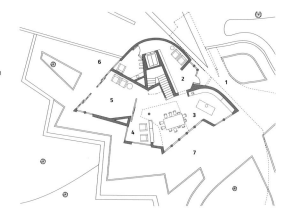

0   2   5 m

27. Maggie's Hong Kong

Tuen Mun Hospital
Tsing Chung Koon Road,
Tuen Mun, N.T.,
Hong Kong, China

Mon - Fri / 9 am - 5 pm

+852 2465 6006
info@maggiescentre.org.hk
www.maggiescentre.org.hk

Located at the western end of a huge modern hospital, Maggie's Hong Kong was Maggie's first international centre. Evoking traditional Chinese architecture, it is composed of pavilions in a range of different shapes and materials, with pitched metal roofs, two of which are bright red. As we come closer, we are slowly immersed in a peaceful oasis with a landscaped garden and two shallow ponds designed by Lily Jencks who was inspired by her mother Maggie Keswick Jencks, a lover of Chinese gardens. When we reach the street entrance, one of the pavilions, almost as a sign of welcome, invites us to enter.

Inside, the luminous spaces of the communal pavilions, large and generous, alternate with more private orange and green consultation rooms, enclosed and contained. Drawn towards the heart of the building, we join people living with cancer around the kitchen table, a 'still point' set among the dynamic spaces of the welcome area, activity room and kitchen. Closely connected with nature, all these spaces interact with the outside through large glass façades providing views of water and sky and the paths towards the gardens: moving from the entrance, a little wooden bridge leads us to the third consultation room (the "blue room") which stands independently in the middle of the pond; exiting the back, another path leads us to the Chinese rock sitting alone at the bottom of the garden.

↗
Maggie's Hong Kong, 2013. Surrounded by water, in the middle of a landscaped garden, the centre rises between two shallow ponds, a bigger one in front of the balcony outside the large sitting room and a smaller one on the back, in the middle to which stands out, isolated, the "blue room"

© Gehry Partners, LLP

architects
Frank Gehry

landscape architect
Lily Jencks

construction
2012 - 2013

1. Entrance
2. Welcome area / Library
3. Office
4. Kitchen
5. Consultation rooms
6. Large sitting room /
   Group activity room
7. Garden
8. Terrace
9. Chinese rock
10. Pond

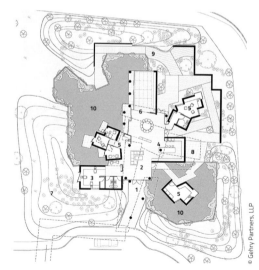

0 2   5 m

© Gehry Partners, LLP

↖
Connected with the entrance pavilion by a little wooden bridge, the "blue consultation room" is detached from the main building

↑
In front of us, the kitchen table, surrounded by the welcome area, kitchen and large sitting room / group activity room constitutes the heart of the building

→
In close connection with nature, all these spaces interact with the outside through large glass façades with views of the water and the sky

28. Maggie's Tokyo

6-4-18 Toyosu, Koto-ku,
Tokyo 135-0061,
Japan

Mon - Fri / 10 am - 4 pm

+81 3 3520 9913
soudan@maggiestokyo.org
www.maggiestokyo.org

Although not located directly within the grounds of a hospital due to the scarcity of available land within the Japanese health system, Maggie's Tokyo is well located and easy to reach from several nearby cancer hospitals. On approaching the site, we appreciate the landscape outside the centre, which is cared for by the people of the community, and leads seamlessly to the small garden inside the centre. The grassy courtyard enclosed between the main building and its annex welcomes us, providing a sense of protection. Set opposite one another, the two buildings with their transparent walls and windows convey an open feeling offering us views of the warm atmosphere inside. On entering, we are struck by a pleasant fragrance from the wooden rooms and the kitchen tabletop built from a 300-year-old tree donated by a supporter. Open and flexible, the space can be divided into smaller rooms with sliding paper screens. From the inside, the views extend beyond the small courtyard to a flower garden that features seed-balls planted twice a year by the local community. After the 2011 Tōhoku earthquake, seed-ball gardening became popular, offering a technique for growing flowers that are cut and arranged in bouquets given to the people who visit and work at Maggie's as a source of healing, courage and energy.

↗
Maggie's Tokyo, 2016.
The centre consists of two separate buildings: the main building (by Cosmos More) and the reused annex (by Nikken Sekkei Ltd) connected by the turfed courtyard (all coordinated by Tsutomu Abe). The roof of the main building is made of the same material as the annex, enhancing a sense of unity

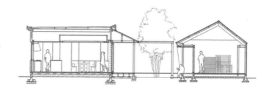

architects
Cosmos More and Nikken
Sekkei Ltd. coordinated by
Tsutomu Abe

landscape architect
Daiichi Engei and Japan
Association of Professional
Garden Designers and
Green Works coordinated
by Yumiko Sato

construction
2016

1. Entrance
2. Welcome area
3. Kitchen
4. Office
5. Toilets
6. Consultation rooms
7. Turfed courtyard
8. Exterior group activity room
9. Library

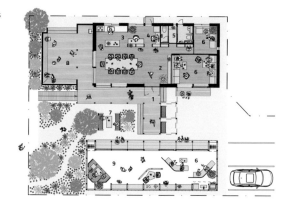

0   2   5 m

↖
Equally spaced, the columns of the external corridor (main building) and of the veranda (annex) form a small courtyard open on one side. Sitting in the shade, visitors can enjoy the view of the garden (by Daiichi Engei) and the landscape around the centre (cared for by the local community)

↑
The wooden interior gives off a pleasant scent. Thanks to the transparency, the visitors of the two buildings feel part of the same space and can communicate with each other

→
The top of the kitchen table, made of 300-year-old tree donated by a supporter, helps Maggie's visitors feel peace of mind

Timeline

1996		Edinburgh			Nottingham	
2002		Glasgow The Gatehouse			Swansea	
2003		Dundee	**2013**		Newcastle	
2005		Highlands			Aberdeen	
2006		Fife			Hong Kong	
2008		West London	**2014**		Oxford	
2010		Cheltenham			Lanarkshire	
2011		Glasgow	**2016**		Tokyo	

Manchester

2017 Forth Valley

 Oldham

 Barts – London
(City & East)

2019 Cardiff

 Yorkshire

 The Royal
Marsden

Kálida Barcelona

2021 Southampton

... **In development**

The Royal Free

Northampton

Coventry

Tauton

Cambridge

Liverpool

Bristol

Norway

Netherlands

Maggie's to Maggie's

"Maggie's to Maggie's" is a walk between some or all centres to raise funds for people with cancer. In addition to helping the organisation, attendees will have the opportunity to enjoy some of the best landscapes in the UK, as well as experience the sensory space of Maggie's centres.

	Highlands	Aberdeen	Dundee	Fife	Forth Valley	Edinburgh	Lanarkshire	Glasgow	Newcastle	Yorkshire
Highlands	—	164	212	238	241	243	261	272	446	591
Aberdeen	164	—	113	153	200	200	227	238	402	557
Dundee	212	113	—	53	90	92	117	129	292	447
Fife	238	153	53	—	55	40	80	92	243	447
Forth Valley	241	200	90	55	—	77	27	39	219	357
Edinburgh	243	200	92	40	77	—	58	77	193	352
Lanarkshire	261	227	117	80	27	58	—	23	235	332
Glasgow	272	238	129	92	39	77	23	—	249	346
Newcastle	446	402	292	243	219	193	235	249	—	159
Yorkshire	591	557	447	447	357	352	332	346	159	—
Manchester	602	566	457	417	367	365	341	356	256	100
Oldham	604	568	518	418	369	364	343	362	224	61
Nottingham	695	660	552	510	462	447	436	449	259	114
Cheltenham	787	753	644	602	554	552	528	542	426	274
Cambridge	822	787	679	637	589	575	563	576	386	248
Oxford	853	800	692	650	602	599	576	589	435	274
Cardiff	880	845	726	687	636	634	610	624	513	367
The Royal Free	892	858	758	703	658	703	658	653	632	652
Barts – London (City & East)	900	866	756	716	666	658	641	658	455	315
West London	909	875	766	724	657	674	650	663	455	332
Swansea	941	906	798	756	708	707	682	695	581	372
Southampton	988	943	827	769	760	744	727	739	584	409
The Royal Marsden	1001	892	840	782	772	756	740	753	546	378
Barcelona	2371	2337	2227	2173	2137	2123	2111	2124	1930	1795
Tokyo	9114	9082	9175	9204	9244	9230	9262	9271	9275	9382
Hong Kong	9457	9573	9460	9484	9531	9502	9547	9563	9481	9547